James P. Beymer
1958.

THE UNSILENT GENERATION

THE UNSILENT GENERATION

*An Anonymous Symposium
in Which Eleven College
Seniors Look at Themselves
and Their World*

COMPILED AND EDITED WITH A FOREWORD BY

OTTO BUTZ

RINEHART & COMPANY, INC.   NEW YORK   TORONTO

Published simultaneously in Canada by
Clarke, Irwin & Company, Ltd., Toronto

© 1958 by Otto Butz
Printed in the United States of America
All rights reserved
Library of Congress Catalog Card Number: 58-6051

To the Class of '57

Editor's Foreword

WHAT IS THE YOUNGER GENERATION of Americans really like?
Approximately how many Americans there will be in the next
twenty years we know. But what kind of men and women
will they be? What will they believe in? What will be their
ambitions, their doubts, and their hopes? What, as human
beings and in their future roles as citizens of a democracy,
can we and the world expect of them?

These questions have, in recent years, occasioned very
considerable speculation. The conclusions most often reached,
however, have unfortunately been anything but reassuring. If,
indeed, we accept the word of a number of popular social
scientists, theologians, and even educators, the young men and
women of America would seem to be a rather unpromising
lot. Taken as a group, we have been told, they are smug, complacent, superficial, lacking in the capacity for idealism, and
characterized by a haunting, if unconscious, sense of emptiness.

But is this really so? Or are these pessimistic diagnoses,
for all their sophistication and eloquence, perhaps merely another case of a misunderstanding between peoples, in this case
between different generations of Americans? Must one not,
in judging the young people of today, remember that the
world in which they have grown up is in a great many important ways a very different one from what it was even two
or three decades ago? Is it not highly unrealistic, not to say

unfair, to expect such qualities as sensitiveness, altruism, and inner stability and direction to be expressed by today's youth in the same outward forms of behavior as were meaningful and in vogue a generation ago? How, for example, does a young American of today intelligently, responsibly, and effectively show his commitment to such ideals as peace, freedom, and the welfare of mankind? Certainly not, as was the respectable and even prestigeful custom in the 1930's, by signing long petitions, by parading about with placards, or by fighting in somebody else's civil war. But does this necessarily mean that today's young American does not share, and is not deeply concerned about implementing, the same basic and traditional American ideals in question? Is it not perhaps the case, in other words, that in judging America's younger generation, it is the older generation, the judges themselves, who are guilty of superficiality, smugness, and an inability to transcend their own particular historical idiom?

It was with questions such as these in mind that I undertook the small, private project which has resulted in the present book. When, in 1949, I first arrived in the United States to do graduate work, my German background and Canadian education in a number of ways inclined me to accept some of the more pessimistic predictions about the American younger generation. Gradually, however, my experiences both as a student and as a teacher in this country caused me to reexamine my earlier reactions. Finally, in February of 1957, it occurred to me that my position as a professor at an American university—Princeton—might enable me to elicit some rather basic documentation on the matter from a source which up to then had hardly been consulted. Why not, I asked myself, let the younger generation at last speak about and for itself?

But exactly how to do this? An opinion poll seemed out of the question. In the first place, I lacked the necessary time and resources; and secondly, I suspected, it would not yield the kind of spontaneous, volunteered, and between-the-lines information that would be most significant and interesting. What I wanted, as much as possible, was a collection of individual, personal statements, addressed to a very general common theme, which each contributing student would be free to interpret and develop as he himself saw fit. And, above all, if the statements were to serve their purpose, they would have to be as honest, searching and frank as the writers could and were prepared to make them. In order, therefore, both to remove as many inhibitions as possible and to discourage the temptation on the part of the authors merely to indulge in personal publicity, I decided right at the beginning on the need for strict anonymity. With these general specifications in mind, I typed up the following paragraph of instructions:

> Write a fifteen to twenty-five typed-page essay on the following theme: *What do you want out of life? What do you want to contribute to life? How has your background affected you in this? What do you think of happiness, success, security, God, education, marriage, family, and your own generation? What, if any, moral problems have you encountered or do you expect to have to face? How do you relate yourself to America's future and to the future of mankind in general?* Try to compose what you put down into as well-organized and literate an essay as possible. Be as honest and thoughtful in what you write as you can. The title for each essay will, where possible, be some phrase, taken from the text, which seems to sum up the particular essay's substance or spirit. //

I had decided that the ideal number of essays for the short collection I envisaged would be twelve. Equipped, therefore, with twelve copies of the above paragraph, I repaired, on several successive afternoons, to Princeton's crowded undergraduate Student Center. Since, with the small number of essays I was soliciting, I could not possibly pretend to any scientifically representative sample, I resigned myself, quite frankly, to operating by rule of thumb: From among the students I had met, either in lectures, seminars, or socially, I would, without any other conscious criteria, select at random twelve who struck me as more or less ordinary Princeton seniors and who, to the extent I could tell, would likely be literate and conscientious enough to be able to write the desired essays and have them completed by graduation.

I at first feared that I would have difficulty both in interesting twelve reliable contributors and then in persuading them to keep their deadline. In both regards I was mistaken. Each of the twelve students whom I approached, once I had explained to him the purposes of the project, seemed genuinely interested and even enthusiastic. The general reaction, as I ran into the boys on campus while they were at work on their essays, was that this sort of thing wasn't easy if one took it seriously, that it was good for a man's soul, and that it was something that everyone should be given an opportunity to experience. By graduation time only one of the twelve boys— because of illness—had not come through.

When I first enlisted the contributors to this collection, I knew well only two of them. Since then all of them have become my friends. As each man completed his piece, my wife and I invited him up to our apartment for refreshments and some discussion about himself and life in general. By a month before graduation, when most of the essays had been handed in, the Saturday-evening sessions had become a regular institution. By ten o'clock the contributors, an occasional girlfriend and relative, and a few close friends would be seated around the room in the most lively, frank, and serious bull sessions (on everything from God to the latest news) that one could possibly wish for. In the beginning, as each boy arrived in the apartment for the first time, they all looked and sounded very much alike—typical "Princeton men." An hour and two drinks later, they were all young Americans, each very much an individual in his own right—prep-school boys and high-school boys; Northerners, Midwesterners and Texans; good students and average students; rich boys and boys from modest backgrounds; future businessmen, professionals and politicians; Catholics, Jews, and Protestants.

In any scientific, statistical sense these essays cannot, of course, claim to be representative, either of the younger generation of Americans as a whole or even of the undergraduate body of Princeton University. Nor are some of the motivations, ideas and experiences of these young men wholly admirable. Yet whatever one may think of the substance of what these American citizens of the future have written about themselves and their world, there is one quality which one cannot deny them: a truly remarkable capacity for self-awareness and an uncompromising insistence on honesty with themselves. It is, of course, an inevitable expression of this quality that in these essays are to be found a number of admissions, statements, and reflections which many a reader may find embarrassing and even disturbing. My own net reaction, nevertheless, is one of profound encouragement.

American society as a whole is undoubtedly one of the best integrated and most smoothly operating of modern history. Unlike the societies of traditional Europe, Americans are agreed upon their fundamentals; and unlike the peoples of the Communist countries, they do not need a system of police terror to enforce them. In the United States, more and more, people of every group and class, the educated and uneducated alike, are all committed members of the system. The intellectual in the sense of the economically, politically or culturally malcontented or alienated individualist, holding up to his society the mirror of awareness and criticism, is, in the United States, increasingly a thing of the past. And while it is this which has helped to make American society as internally secure as it is, it is also a fact which might well prove a long-range danger. For every society, especially one as prosperous and traditionally successful as that of the United States has been, inevitably bears within it the temptation to smugness and the notion that its continued prosperity and success may be taken for granted.

In Europe, where the upbringing and education of the business, professional, and administrative leaders has tended to concentrate on cultural and social traditionalism and exclusiveness, the job of combating this tendency to smugness and complacency has, with more or less success, been performed by the intellectuals. In the United States, I am suggesting, intellectuals in this sense may soon have disappeared altogether. But rather than a loss, this circumstance may, very possibly, turn out to be a unique gain. *For what could be a sounder situation for a society which hopes to remain dynamic, stable, and free than to have the essential function of social criticism, awareness, and soul-searching performed by its businessmen, professionals, and administrators themselves?* It is because these essays (to the extent that they may be representative in this regard at least) would seem to offer the possible prospect of such a development, that I have found them so encouraging. For whatever else the reader may think of these young authors and their essays, on one point he is bound to agree: they are, as a group, *both* ambitious future businessmen, professionals, and administrators *and* determined, aware, and introspective young intellectuals. If and to the extent that they can remain such throughout their lives, their liberal education will have served its purpose and served it well—and the United States and the world will have sounder grounds for confidence in the American future than a good many Americans may have dared to hope.

In concluding this brief foreword I must mention that the idea for this undertaking was wholly my own, that I at no time during its preparation informed or consulted the administration of Princeton University, and that this book has been published without Princeton University's endorsement. For the substance of the essays I and the contributing authors are responsible jointly. And, I might add, whatever royalties should accrue from the sale of the book will be apportioned on the basis of ten per cent to myself, as the editor, the remainder to be divided equally among the respective contributors.

Otto Butz
Princeton, N.J.
June, 1957

Contents

THE UNSILENT GENERATION

SO HERE I AM

BEFORE I TELL YOU ABOUT MYSELF, I think I'll introduce you to my family. That way, maybe you'll understand me a bit better. My father—my real father, that is—was in his late fifties when he married my mother. She was just out of high school and off my grandfather's little farm in East Texas. Why she married him I'll never understand. He had already lived a full life; she still had hers to live. But she did, and so here I am.

Dad was quite a character. He was born in one of the Dakotas—which one I don't think even he knew. While he was still a kid, his father died. Because he was the oldest, and his mother couldn't support all three of her children, he was sent out to earn his keep. He had a hard time of it—he even got buggy-whipped a few times—and he built up some real hate. I gather he ran away, because at the next stage of his life I know of he was riding the ranges in Kansas, I think. This was a rather colorful period—at least once he even got himself shot at. (He was fooling with another man's girl, just because the other fellow had told him not to.) Next, he served an apprenticeship as a watchmaker and then set himself up as a watchmaker and jeweler in a Southern coastal city. He was an excellent watchmaker. He probably forgot more than most watchmakers today know (if I may use an old cliché). He apparently developed a fairly good business. He married, had one daughter, whom he sent to a good Southern girls' school, and built himself a fine house. However, some time in the late Twenties, his business failed. For a while, too, his family life had not been satisfactory. So he and his wife were divorced, and he left with effectively nothing. He teamed up with a friend of his, leasing land in East Texas, in the hope that oil would be found on it. The other man supplied the capital, and Dad did the leg work. It was at this time that he met my mother.

Mother was the third of eight children. Her family lived on a small East Texas farm. And believe me, they lived hard. To eke a living out of that damn clay, every one of them had to pitch in. Mother went to grade school in a little one-room schoolhouse near the farm. A pretty rural place, I gather. And later, when she went to town to high school, she was treated as one of the country hicks. Apparently she was, too. The five miles into town by wagon and team was quite a distance. And that's how she remembers traveling it. The town and country were really separate. I think the way Mother was treated in high school has a lot to do with her marrying Dad. When she finished high school, she continued living in town with some relatives, and took a job as an elevator operator. It was on this job that she met Dad. She was apparently quite impressed with his showing any interest in her. So against her family's wishes, she married him. I consider this to be the greatest mistake she ever made in her life. But I suppose I shouldn't condemn it too much as, without it, I wouldn't be.

Before I was old enough really to be aware of much, we moved far from East Texas to another little town. The reason for the move was Dad's poor health. And this other town was where I grew up. We had a little house not too far from the school, and a nice lawn where I could play. Things seemed really rosy to me. But they weren't. Until recently I never knew it, but we were really quite poor. All we had was the small income from the oil-land leases Dad had worked out, plus what Mother made as a waitress. Dad could have found himself a job as a jeweler, but because he wanted to maintain the façade that he was a "retired" man, he just puttered around in his garden.

Mother and Dad didn't have a stable marriage. It seems obvious to me now that they never could have had one. When I was eight, they were divorced. Mother told the court that she did not want custody of me. What the court didn't know was that Dad had told her that if she tried to take me, he'd kill us both. And he probably would have. A few days after Mother left, she married another man, whom she'd met working as a waitress. I can't blame her for leaving. Dad made life pretty tough for her. But I can't help feeling cheated. I lost a mother when I needed one most, and I completely lack the sense of security and companionship which people have who have had a real family. And I can never really know or love my mother as I could if I had had her in those years.

Dad never forgave Mother for leaving him. And he figured the best way to get back at her was through me. He began almost immediately from the time she left to indoctrinate me against her. Seven years later, when he died, I had been thoroughly "brainwashed." At that time I would not have gone to live with my mother under any circumstances.

Dad loved me a great deal and was very good to me. While he disciplined me severely and had many chores for me, he gave me everything he could. I loved him a great deal, too. And I respected him. Besides instilling in me the desire "to get ahead," he drilled into me principles of honesty and ethical behavior. Unfortunately, as I know now, he didn't always obey these rules himself. I will always love him, but I can never have the respect for him I once had.

Dad's death brought many complications. I was firmly decided not to go to live with my mother. Now in order to assure that Mother would never get me, Dad had had my half sister adopt me. So on his death, she and her worthless (in my opinion) husband came out, I think, to see what they could get. What they found were a lot of debts, and very little else. Anyway, I had no intention of leaving the little town where I had grown up. I hadn't bothered to figure out how I was going to manage this, but I knew I was. At this time, in what was really the darkest moment, help came from an unexpected quarter. The Edwards family offered me a home. So I was adopted by the Edwardses and went to live with them.

The Edwards family is completely different from anything else in my background. They really were a family unit. And they were well educated. Mr. Edwards is a Princeton man, and Mrs. Edwards, in addition to having graduated from the best college in the state, is a prodigious reader. Besides Mr. and Mrs. Edwards, whom I now call Dad and Mother, there was a boy, Bill, who was one year ahead of me, and a girl, Ann, two years behind me. The emphasis in this family was much different from that in my previous "family." My real father had stressed making more money than anyone else, and showing it. What mattered most with the Edwards family was people—living with them and helping them. What they did for me is a good example. And there was something else that the Edwardses stressed—superior performance on the job. While we kids were in high school, where good marks came easily, this expectation never showed up. Once we got to college we could feel it unmistakably.

Mr. Edwards is one of the finest men I have ever known. He's a successful businessman, and very competent in his work. But what I find really outstanding about him is the way he helps people all around him. Ever since I have known him he has been supporting, at least partially, one family or more in addition to his own. In a way, I look at him as a giant, carrying everyone else along on his coattails. This is not to say that I think he is without faults; I just find his faults trivial.

Mrs. Edwards I idealize a little less. She's a fine, educated woman, and has very friendly manners. But she tends to be domineering. (She was especially so towards us children.) She can be very stubborn, sarcastic, and even condescending. These qualities, combined with her keen intelligence, can be incredibly cutting. And she has a fabulous temper. No sane man would stand in her way when she is angry. Still, it is primarily because of her that the Edwards family has the orientation towards other people that it does. She is a devout Catholic, who will have both strong Faith and many Works on her record when she knocks at the Gate. She built up the local library practically singlehanded. And she is the driving force that keeps it going. Yet she's never been paid a cent for it. I should point out that, even though I may realize her shortcomings, just as I saw those of my real father, I know that I am very much in debt to this second mother of mine—and I do love her.

Bill Edwards was a boy whom I knew well long before I became his foster brother. He's quite intelligent, and just a shade conceited. But he has plenty to be conceited about. Besides being president and valedictorian of his class, he was the school photographer, a first-rate debater, and the best trumpet player the school ever had. In short, he had a really great high-school record—a record which is based entirely on his own competence and which he built up in spite of the fact that he has a rather cold personality. Until I got to college Bill Edwards was my ideal. Because I admired his intelligence and abilities so much, I found myself imitating not only his hobbies but even his reserved personality.

Ann is just the opposite. She's bright, too. But where Bill is a worker, she's lazy. Consequently, she never built up the spectacular record that Bill did. However, as long as she doesn't overeat (as she likes to), she is and will stay a very pretty girl. And pretty girls, I guess, don't need a record of special achievement.

The years I spent with the Edwardses I look on as the happiest of my life. And they have been among the most important, too, certainly as far as my intellectual development has been concerned. And of course, if it hadn't been for Mr. Edwards, I would never have applied to a first-class college—if I'd gone to college at all. It was through him, and through him alone, that I became interested in Princeton.

These, briefly, have been the major characters in my life. Now let me see what I can tell you about myself.

Physically, I'm a little, nervous, thin fellow. I look much younger than I am. (People often take me for a freshman or a high-school student.) I feel sure that I'm intelligent—or else I wouldn't be at Princeton. I'm not poised at all. So among people whom I don't know very well I'm usually rather quiet. This gives the impression that I'm shy. Actually, I don't think I'm shy. I just can't think of anything worth saying—so I don't say anything. I have a tremendous drive (to do just what, I'm not sure) which enables me to work very hard and a great deal. During my four years at Princeton I have probably had an average work week of about seventy hours. This, combined with the fact that my department marks high, will enable me to graduate in the upper quarter of my class.

I don't know exactly where this is leading me. Originally I thought I wanted to get rich. But now I find myself more interested in science. If I go into science, I know that I'll never be lacking a comfortable living, but I also know that I will never have a great deal of wealth. The fact is that I'm not quite sure just what I want from life. Actually, now I tend to consider more what I'm capable of *doing* rather than what I *want*. I would like to have enough money to be comfortable and somewhat well-to-do. Beyond that it doesn't make any difference. I'd only give it away, anyway, either before or after I die— probably before, so that I could enjoy doing it. What else is it good for?

But I do want something out of life which I can consider as evidence that I am better than average—an ego booster, if you please. When I say "better," I don't mean in the social sense, or on account of my family, or anything like that. "Better" to me means more competent, more capable. The best man, to me, is the one who does the job best, regardless of who his family is or whom he knows. I want to be more capable than the mediocre masses, whom I despise because of their apathy and mediocrity. This is why I work as I do. To ensure that I will never fall into those masses.

In life the thing I value most is happiness, which to me is roughly material comfort. I not only want this f _ myself, but also for the rest of the world. This is one of the reasons I am a scientist—so I can chip in my two bits' worth towards the well-being of the rest of the world. If during my lifetime I make the rest of humanity, or humanity to come, just one iota more comfortable, then I will be content.

From a purely personal point of view, what I want is a position where I do the kind of work I'm interested in. I want a comfortable, friendly home where I can hang my hat, with a wife I can love, and be loved by, a couple of kids, and a dog whose ears I can scratch. Home to me will be a place I can come to tired, and where I can be at peace with the world.

And where, I've sometimes been asked, does God fit into this scheme of mine? The truth is that religion has become a very touchy subject with me. When I look at the world around me, I find it difficult to conceive of an omnipotent, all-good, fatherlike deity. Such a deity wouldn't permit the pain and suffering that exists. It seems to me that deity can be all-good and fatherlike only if he is infinite. But if he is really infinite, he must be very sadistic to allow the things he does. The argument that God tortures us to test our faith is so much bull to me, because if he's truly infinite, he *knows* how we will react. He doesn't need to test the faith of tiny infants in India by letting them starve to death! I prefer to believe in no god at all rather than in this kind of a god. And any finite god that exists seems to be quite inert, at least to me. The universe seems pretty well to function regularly, in the manner which science has described. Maybe God just triggered everything, and then sat back on his haunches to watch. I figure I can be indifferent to an indifferent god.

There are other aspects of the concept of deity that disturb me. Where did he come from? Wouldn't one have to consider an omnipotent deity morally responsible for all the evil in the world, since he has the power to prevent, and foresees it? If I know a dog is vicious, and I release him from a chain, I'm held responsible for the damage he does. Aren't people who cause damage in our world analagous to the dog, since omnipotent deity could restrain them? All these things bothered me long before I came to Princeton. I used to sit in church and worry about them. In high school I attended church quite regularly—twice every Sunday, plus Sunday school. I wanted to believe. I wanted to believe very much. I used to pray—just pray for an answer, a sign that I could have faith in, or for faith itself. That's all over now. Before I finished high school I was aware of the logical paradoxes which riddle the Christian religion, and I was nearly saturated with doubt about the existence of God. I still don't know, but now I've decided that I can't wait for the answer. There may be a God, and there may not. I'm inclined to say there isn't. But rather than worry about this, the practical problem before me is to work out a way of life—a *modus vivendi* of some sort with the world. So far as religion goes, what I want now is to be left alone.

It seems to me a bit ironic that even with such mixed-up religious views, I find myself living by stronger, harder prin-

ciples than most of the faithful Christians I know. I accepted
a job offer in my junior year, and then received another offer
with a considerably higher salary from another company.
Several good Christian friends suggested I take the second
offer and dump the first company. The idea horrified me, and
still does. I think a man's word should be as good as his signature on a legal contract. I like to be able to trust people, and I
like to be trusted. If the so-called Christians around me would
stick to their professed principles, then I *would* trust them.
But they don't. Christians often seem to ignore the Golden
Rule unless they know the other person to some degree, and
even then they don't rigorously stick to it. Their sexual morality
is a farce; and business ethics, except in one or two closely
knit professions, have to be codified into law. If people would
stick to their professed principles, *this* world could be a much
better one. And it is *this* world, not the next one, that I'm concerned with.

Go ahead! Call me a blind, foolish idealist. I am. I know
that I am. If I weren't, I wouldn't adhere to the things I think
are right, without even hope of reward after death, and the
certainty of no reward in this world. Perhaps I'm just in-
hibited. Perhaps going to church so long brainwashed me.
This is probably the case. Consequently I would like to marry
a girl who really is a Christian—who really sticks to her principles—and to send my children to church, just as I went.
Then maybe they'll be brainwashed, too.

Supposedly, any frank autobiography, in order to be complete, must contain a vivid description of one's sex life. So I
suppose I ought to give it at least a line or two. I can count
the number of times in my life that I have "necked" with a girl
on my fingers (of one hand, if you please). I have never had
intercourse, and I don't intend to until I am married. I feel
that it's wrong. Furthermore, I want to marry a girl who is a
virgin, and I think that it would be grossly unfair of me to

demand that she be something that I am not. While I find that most of the striving of women for "equality" is actually a disguised effort to expand their already preferential status, I think that in this respect they're not getting a fair deal. The double standard just isn't right. It's got to be everybody either on one standard or the other, but not some on one, and some on the other. I'm for chastity, myself.

Closely analagous are my feelings concerning treatment of the Negroes. I don't think they're getting a fair break, especially from an economic standpoint, and I think they should. Equal schools are essential for this. It is evident that the South will never make them really equal. So I think integration is the only answer. I do, however, object to the Supreme Court's *telling* us we must integrate. I'd rather see the states themselves do it, but, of course, that would probably never happen. While I want to see the Negroes have an equal opportunity for economic and academic achievement and the like, I don't give a hang what happens to them socially (just as I don't care what happens to anyone else socially). I'm totally indifferent to whether or not there happens to be a Negro at the party I go to. I'm not going out of my way to get one there. He'll have to bring himself. On the other hand, like a true Southerner, my dander rises over intermarriage. This I oppose violently for purely emotional reasons. And I'd pull the whole works down to prevent it.

When I come right down to it, I think I have two conflicting goals in life—achievement and security. I'm ambitious in that I want respect for the work that I do. I want to rise in status as far as my abilities will carry me. But I'm a coward when it comes to taking a chance. I don't want to gamble. What I want is a stable order of things in which I can work without exposing myself to ruin.

Princeton has given me one such order. There are only

two factors in academic achievement—intelligence and hard work. Since nearly everyone at Princeton has exceptional intelligence, work is the primary means of differentiation between students here. There are only a few people here who are so much smarter than the rest of us that they can make top grades with little work. Hard work is something I do well.

Because I need a stable order in which to operate, I dislike people who break the rules of the order. Because I am a worker, I dislike the loafers who do not produce to the maximum of their ability. There are a number of such people at Princeton. I call them "hackers." They are the people who do a minimum of work and who simply pursue their own enjoyment—often recklessly and at the expense of others. They are the students who get drunk and smash windows, destroy the janitors' tools, and throw beer cans down the stairs. (Have you ever tried to concentrate with beer cans clattering down the stairs outside your door?) And whom do these people blame when they're punished for what they do? It's all the fault of the fellow who reported them or of the Dean who is obviously biased and doesn't understand their side. With these people I have no sympathy. If they don't want to stick to the system, then I favor getting rid of them. Fortunately at Princeton they are a small minority.

Many people claim to be entirely self-made. I would like to be able to claim this, but it simply is not so. I have already had at least two major breaks in my life. Harsh as it may seem to say it, the first of these was my real father's death, which threw me into the Edwards family. This made possible the second—my admission to Princeton. This in turn now leads on to greater possibilities—to graduate studies and a Ph.D., and from there probably to another "secure order" in a company hierarchy, the draft board willing. Princeton has given me just what I came here to get—a good, solid education.

Well, maybe now you understand a little bit about me,

and what makes me tick. There's really nothing extraordinary to me except for a mixed-up family background, and unorthodox religious views. In a roomful of people you'd never notice me. But it takes just plain people to keep the world going.

A GENTLEMAN'S SON

WHEN, ON MY FOURTEENTH BIRTHDAY, my father dropped me off at the expensive preparatory school which I was to attend for four years, he took leave of me with these final words: "You are a gentleman and a gentleman's son, and don't ever forget it." That admonition has stuck in my mind ever since.

What did my father mean by a "gentleman"? He meant a man with self-respect and independence of judgment. He meant a man well trained in both his mind and his body. He meant a man accomplished in the social graces; a man, for example, who knows his wines, can hold his liquor, and doesn't feel ill at ease when faced at the dinner table with a ten-piece place-setting.

My home life, in spirit as well as in detail, has been a conscious and unconscious cultivation of this ideal. In the exclusive suburb of the Midwestern metropolis where we live, for example, there are no business buildings, stores, gas stations, or anything else which might detract from the beauty of the well-tended homes. We have no police force, fire department, or city government of any form. Our informal town commission has stipulated that in the deed of every home there be a clause which obligates the owner not to sell his property to a Negro or Jew. My parents belong to the country club, the athletic club, the university club, and other social organizations whose membership is restricted to the acceptable people in the area. Until I went to preparatory school I had never really known any Jewish individuals. I had gathered that they were the sort of people one stayed away from. My home environment is of the type that ninety-nine per cent of the nation has been taught to hate and resent.

My father is a Southern gentleman from a prominent family with a proud and rich heritage. He believes, above all, that everyone should behave in a manner befitting his background. He has become a wealthy manufacturer who attributes his success to diligent work and an imaginative mind. After seeing my father on the job, I agree with his thesis that the eight-hour day and the forty-hour week are the luxury of labor, not of management. I have often driven him to the office on a Saturday or found him dictating in the study on Sunday afternoons. Since he is a very active person, who loves his business, I'm positive that he will never be able to accept the leisure of retirement. He will probably meet his Maker while busily occupied at his highly polished mahogany desk.

Father believes that all men should be considered equal and be given equal opportunity for educational and economic advancement. Socially he is somewhat less flexible. He believes, too, that while individuals should have equal opportunity for advancement, they should also be prepared to accept the risks and consequences of failure; they should not, in other words, expect some divine force, *i.e.*, the government, to rescue them from their plight. He is convinced that Franklin D. Roosevelt, through his "levelling" policies, has upset the natural social order of the United States and is, therefore, the greatest traitor in our history.

With my father being the practical and severe business-man that he is, my mother, fortunately, is the direct antithesis. A Grosse Pointe debutante and a Vassar graduate, she is a charming, attractive and very feminine woman, who has a warm smile and a kind word for everyone. While she knows absolutely nothing about business and can't understand my father's deep concern over a two-point drop in the market, she has the no less valuable virtues of being a perfect hostess, a marvellous bridge player, and an ideal instructor in the social graces for her two sons. She has a passion for Hattie Carnegie hats, Jacques Fath originals and Joy perfume, and loves parties, caviar and the Junior League. Her biggest disappointment in life, I suspect, has been the fact that she didn't have a daughter, who would, of course, have had the grandest debutante party in the city's history.

But all this is not to say that my mother is a frivolous, empty-headed socialite. On the contrary, she has performed two functions for our family which have in no wise been less important than what has been contributed by my father. For one thing, she has been our Mother. Although I now consider myself my father's son, my mother was much closer to me in my earlier life. It was she who cleaned me up for birthday parties, who took me to Sunday school, and who, with an approving smile, watched me—at the tender age of eleven—try to maneuver a girl three inches taller than myself around a slippery dance floor. At that time, as far as I was concerned, Dad was merely a big, gruff-voiced man in a business suit.

Aside from thus rearing a family of which my father is very proud, my mother has, I believe, been one of the primary reasons for my father's business success. Many has been the time when she has sympathized with his problems, encouraged him by having faith in his decisions, and—when she thought necessary—figuratively given him a good swift kick in the seat of the pants. All this has convinced me that a wife can easily make or break her husband in his career, and that a man, when choosing his wife, should always carefully bear this in mind.

The other person in my family who has affected my character and thinking has been my older brother. He is a very colorful, professional playboy, who has three main character-istics: firstly, a loathing of work; secondly, a love of fun and excitement; and thirdly, an inheritance of several million dollars —which makes it possible for him to afford the former two characteristics. My brother didn't have a job until he was thirty. And the only reason he finally got one—as an invest-ment banker—was that my father was making life miserable for him and calling him an unemployed vagrant.

In his choice of his first wife my brother showed very poor judgment. He married a truly despicable woman, who refused to accept him as he was and, instead, tried to reform him. When she failed at this, she adopted three apparent goals —incessantly nagging him, being nasty to my family, and lavishly spending his money. He finally rid himself of this parasite in a spectacular divorce, and is now married to a sympathetic blonde heiress. She, too, in her slower and more understanding way, is trying to convince him of the virtues of earning a living. Since he loves this woman, and idolizes his five children, she may well achieve some gradual success in her efforts. Yet even so, in his capacity as an investment banker, my brother seems unlikely either to add much to his fortune or to develop many ulcers. And I expect that he will retire early. His real interests in life will probably continue to be those of his long playboy youth—flying, yachting, sports-car racing, and well-liquored pleasure trips to Europe and Jamaica.

I know that many people would criticize my brother for his lack of productiveness and would feel that he should be trying to contribute to life more positively. Although I per-sonally would have embarked on a different road if I had inherited as much money as he did, I feel that a man has the prerogative to do with his life what he wants, without having to answer for his choice to anyone. The secret of happiness, I believe, is to be true to oneself—and the rest of the world can go to hell.

As far as my own thinking goes, I believe it reflects to a considerable degree the thinking of each of these other members of my family. I have inherited my father's business sense, my mother's social awareness, and my brother's flamboyancy. Adding to this such native intelligence as I have, plus my Princeton education, I am now confidently looking forward to entering the world of big business. I have chosen this field of endeavor because I think it offers the greatest and most exciting challenge as well as the richest rewards by way of money, prestige, and general self-satisfaction.

My choice of a job will be based on the following considerations. Firstly, I want the job which will offer me the greatest opportunity for rapid advancement. And, because I feel, frankly, that there is no hurdle too high for me, I am anxious to have my advancement based strictly on merit and value to the company. Secondly, I want a position that is lucrative. My own tastes are discriminating, and so will likely be those of my family. I want to be able to afford whatever I and my family may desire. At no time do I ever intend to apologize for these tastes; I would be extremely critical if any member of my family ever suggested "keeping down with the Joneses." And thirdly, I want as rapidly as possible to attain a position of real responsibility. The reason for this is that I am the kind of person who performs best when the risks are great, and the job to be done and the decisions to be made are important and really count.

In the search for a career in which I could live according to these expectations of mine, I have, in the past several months, anxiously had myself interviewed by more than a dozen different companies. These interviews have suddenly brought home to me more clearly than ever before that there are disadvantages as well as advantages to being a polished, confident and aggressive Ivy Leaguer. I found that as I talked with the representatives of the smaller and more conservative and provincial companies, I inevitably detected a feeling, on the part of the interviewer, of resentment and sometimes even of animosity towards me. When, on the other hand, I was being looked over by the really large and dynamic enterprises, the situation was exactly the opposite. I walked into the room, the representative shook my hand, and both of us would immediately feel a sense of easy rapport. The reason for this, as I quickly realized, was, of course, that the progressive corporations with the truly big potential are the ones which staff their top executive levels with my kind of person. What this reflects on the part of the corporations in question, it seems to me, is simply a realistic recognition of the fact that, more and more, the American business, governmental, as well as educational elite is coming to consist of people like me.

I do not make this observation from a sense of snobbishness. I find, admittedly, that the people I naturally hit it off with are generally of one type. They are, however, in no way restricted by racial, religious, cultural or economic background. My friends are usually intelligent, well-bred, sophisticated, confident and cosmopolitan; the one thing they must never be is "pushers." As a group, our social aspirations might best be described as a life combining the tones of *Holiday* magazine and *Sports Illustrated*. While I confine my personal friendships to individuals of this general type, I find that I dislike almost no one. Most people, true enough, I wouldn't invite for a drink to my country club. But this is not a matter of disliking them or feeling superior to them. We are simply different; intimate social contact would be pointless and probably boring on *both* sides.

There is one type of person, however, who, I find, hates me and my friends. He is generally a man with a social inferiority complex, who is not satisfied with his middle-class status and who envies us. I find that in discussions, business contacts, or social gatherings, I cannot muster the enthusiasm to give this type of individual the feeling that I give a damn about him. This, of course, alienates him even further. But why should he feel insulted? If I didn't represent something he envies, he probably wouldn't be the least bit interested in me. So, since I find him obnoxious, why should I go out of my way to appease him?

While I am on this subject I might add that I believe that, more and more, the elite of the United States is not being determined either by family background or on the basis of inherited wealth. The new criteria, as I see it, are intelligence, good education, a sense of public responsibility, a deep-rooted commitment to Western civilization's basic humanistic values, and a capacity for independent judgment. The men who measure up to these criteria are what I would call America's new liberals. Living in a more obviously complex world, and no longer hounded by the injustices of an earlier day, these liberals share the fundamental values of the liberals of the 1930's, but not, by any means, their simple-minded and self-righteous utopianism. This new type of liberal, it seems to me, is one of the finest achievements that American society has produced. And while he owes his existence to our society's great economic, social and political successes, he is, at the same time, the country's best hope that these successes may continue. A democracy, particularly one with the unavoidable international problems and opportunities of our own, can only survive if it has truly enlightened and responsible leadership. On the one hand, it must transcend the inevitable material and social self-centeredness and provincialism of the democratic masses. On the other hand, it must protect itself against whatever challenges to its order of things may develope from the political extremists, whether of the radical Left or the radical Right. To provide this kind of essential leadership—whether in government, business, or the professions—is the new type of liberal's greatest responsibility.

As I have said, liberals of this type are developed, not born. And I believe that the lead in producing this kind of person is firmly held by universities and colleges such as Princeton. Princeton itself has been the most often and bitterly criticized university in America. It has been called, among other things, a glorified preparatory school and a haven of Communists and fellow travellers. All these criticisms are nonsense; they have originated either with the narrow-minded rich, or with the envious poor and ignorant. The fact of the matter is that, more than ever, Princeton is serving the nation not only by itself training America's future liberal leaders but, no less importantly, by setting an example which can be, and is being, followed by colleges and universities throughout the country.

How does Princeton do this? A recent article in a Midwestern newspaper came up with the finding that all Princetonians look alike, dress alike, talk alike, and think alike. To one unfamiliar with Princeton and only on a brief visit to the campus, the first three of these generalizations may well appear to be true. But the charge that we all think alike is utterly ridiculous. If there is one dominant purpose to which the Princeton liberal-arts education is geared, it is the development of individual and independent thought processes. About *what* one thinks, the university and most of the professors are quite permissive; *that* one think and examine history, the world, and oneself, the university and the faculty insist. And even the students themselves, in their estimation of one another, attach the greatest importance to this inclination and capacity. The highest-prestige students in Princeton's graduating classes may or may not be wealthy, and may or may not conform to the admitted Princeton standards of dress and outward behavior. One thing they may never be, however, is intellectual conformists. As anyone who cares to check up can quickly discover, they are, in fact, almost always among the most intellectually capable and truly independent of the entire student body.

Many critics of Princeton accuse Princetonians of being conceited, snobbish, and brash. There may be something to what these critics are getting at, even though the words they use are inaccurate. I believe that most of us at Princeton do feel ourselves, as a group, to be intellectually superior to almost any other similar group in the country. But is this a matter of snobbishness or merely of realism? When I see that Princeton usually can point to the greatest number of Rhodes Scholars, the highest percentage of graduates (per size of the student body) in *Who's Who,* the highest average results on aptitude tests, and the largest ratio of applications to acceptances, I have to agree that as a group we must in fact *be* superior. But with most of us, I think, this feeling of superiority does not engender what could honestly be called snobbishness. What it does, more than anything, is to act as an impetus and stimulus for us to try to live up to the expectations that we and others have of ourselves as a group. But is this a bad thing?

As far as I myself am concerned, the single factor in my character that has been developed most fully at Princeton is my intellectual self-confidence. Having graduated *cum laude* from prep school, I expected Princeton to be little more than a gymnastic exercise. I never worked as hard in my life, however, as I did during my first Princeton semester; yet with all the work, I found that my grades were just slightly above average. Seeing others who worked much less than I gaining better grades, I finally sat down to analyze what these other individuals had that I lacked. What gave these people their advantage, I soon discovered, was their capacity to ignore the multitude of irrelevant details in courses and books, to search out and concentrate on the real essentials, and then, on the basis of these essentials, to develop thoughts and arguments of their own. By the end of my second freshman semester I, too, had mastered this technique. And ever since, as a result, I, for my part at least, have found Princeton actually to be the country club that it is sometimes reputed to be.

I can honestly say that during my last three years at Princeton, I have spent two fifths of my time on campus, two fifths away having a wonderful time, and the last fifth travelling back and forth. I have made two trips annually to Florida or the Caribbean, and have had only one dateless weekend in three years. Yet with all this galavanting about, I have managed to keep my academic grades well above average. I find, in fact, that if I do well on my final comprehensive examinations, there may even be a Phi Beta Kappa Key within my grasp. If, after the little work I have done, I should be awarded a Key, it would, of course, be a mockery of the whole system. But, I confess, it's just that that makes me look forward to the possibility the most. Towards the people who for four years have actually labored to achieve this honor I feel no malice; but I realize that as far as their attitudes towards me are concerned, they do not always reciprocate this feeling.

Given the kind of person I am, I believe that the most important decision of my life will be my choice of a wife. I feel that what more than anything else makes the difference between an ordinary man and a great man is the woman he is married to. To develop his full capabilities a man must have a wife with a similar outlook on life, similar interests and, above all, similar aspirations. I myself have found such a woman—if she will have me. As far as I am concerned, she's a second Grace Kelly, except that she's more flamboyant.

You might expect that the girl I choose to marry will obviously be a typical Eastern debutante. She is—but not quite. Nancy, a Baltimorean, disappointed her parents by refusing to go to Vassar and, instead, entering a rather casual university in Florida. We met during spring vacation of our freshman year, and fell madly in love. We wanted to get married immediately, but there were some rather weighty deterrents—such as our two sets of parents. So we postponed the formalities. One example of how close we came to eloping occurred on one of the vacations we spent together in Florida. With our last hundred dollars I went to buy our plane tickets back to Baltimore. I noticed that for the same price we could go to Mexico City. We discussed the choice in a cocktail lounge, but decided against it because we were both ill due to the seafood we had eaten the night before.

Nancy and I have developed together both mentally and physically and have established between us what I believe is an unbreakable bond. I find that she has influenced my habits and attitudes as much as any other single factor, including my parents and Princeton. Before I realized it, I too had become a Baltimorean. And because Nancy thought that it would be romantic, I soon found myself quite actively engaged in such elegant pastimes as cricket, beagling, and polo.

During the middle of our junior year everything went sour and we stopped seeing each other. At first I found myself perfectly delighted with my new freedom. That was for about a week. Although I never had any difficulty in finding and occasionally seducing interesting females, I discovered that I had no desire ever to see any of them a second time. Hoping that I could remove that empty feeling in my heart, I dated all kinds of girls. But none of them ever managed to satisfy me intellectually or, for that matter, even physically. (I actually fell asleep beside an anxious Miss America finalist who told me that I was the first person who had ever turned down the opportunity.) My inevitable fate was to attempt a rapprochement with Nancy. Now, after several attempts, we are back together again. If it doesn't work out this time, it never will. But I'm optimistic. Our understanding of each other has become deeper and deeper, and our infatuation with each other is as complete as ever. I imagine that one of these days, after graduation, we will suddenly make up our minds to elope—and none of our parents will be able to produce the grand wedding they want so much.

As far as religion goes, my thoughts are as yet not crystallized. The reason, probably, is that up to now I have not yet felt the need for any kind of divine help or guidance. I seldom think of God as such, and only pray when I am exceptionally troubled. Even when I pray, I don't consider myself to be asking for help or advice. I simply find I derive a measure of comfort and self-assurance. Although I don't know the difference between the creeds of the various Protestant faiths, I am a member of the Episcopal church. The reasons for this are not very profound: my parents had me confirmed as an Episcopalian when I was a boy; most of my close friends are Episcopalians; and I find the Episcopalian services enjoyable. While I seldom attend church now, I realize that it will in all probability assume a greater importance as I grow older.

For the moment, I guess, I'm still an unshaken believer in the motto that life is what you make it. True enough, the world is getting to be more complex with every day that passes. Internationally, the subtleties of power politics make easy and unlimited initiative more and more difficult. And at home, the centralized, democratic welfare state—in one form or another, and under one party or another—seems here to stay. But does this mean, as is so often bewailed, that the individual is doomed? Not at all. At the top and among the big boys, whether in business or in government, the decisions to be made and the risks to be taken are as momentous and challenging as ever. The elite which makes these decisions, and upon whom the future of the world will more and more depend, must and will consist of the kind of intelligent, aggressive, and cosmopolitan-minded liberals whom I have already described. To belong to that new liberal elite, on as close to my own terms as possible, is my principal aim in life.

One last thought. Somewhere, I think it was in a book on sociology, I read about a notion called "the self-fulfilling prophecy." The idea was that if a man believes and prophesies that he is going to fail at something, the mere fact that he *is* pessimistic will weaken him and will tend actually to make his failure all the more likely. If, on the other hand, he is optimistic about his prospects and believes and prophesies that he can succeed, the mere fact that he *is* optimistic will so strengthen him in his efforts that his chances of success are much greater, no matter what the odds. It may be, as some foreigners and our prophets of doom so often tell us, that Americans are most naïve in their optimism and confidence. For myself, as well as for the United States as a nation, however, this optimism and confidence seem to me to be our unique and most valuable strength. The going may be much tougher than we expect, and the results much less ideal than we hope for. But armed with our naïveté, we are going to get a lot further than we would without it. Life, undoubtedly, is not going to turn out exactly what we want to make it. But, at least, we'll leave our imprint on it and it won't be what *others* make it.

SURVIVAL OF THE FITTEST

I LOOK LIKE ONE; I DRESS LIKE ONE; but I am *not* an "Ivy Leaguer." In spite of the convincing outward veneer which I have acquired, deep down inside me I have reacted against the Ivy League Man and all that he stands for. The main reason for this is probably to be found in my background, in my life before I came East to Princeton.

I was born and spent my early childhood in the Midwest, but received my secondary schooling in a large, social high school in California. I come from a middle-class family, my father being one of the millions of white-collar government employees. My family life has been happy and uninterrupted, except for a three-year period during World War II when my father was with the United States Navy in the South Pacific.

I was very young, a third grader, when my father left us stranded in a "tough" neighborhood of a medium-large city. In this section of town, on the *other* side of the railroad tracks, children lived by an old and simple rule, called "survival of the fittest." You had to live by your wits and your fists. This led to scars, but it also led to the formation of gangs for mutual security. We called ours the "Wolf Pack." After a year or two, I joined up with a gang of older guys from the high school. I was smart enough to realize that I would be safest with them. Because I was the youngest, they used me as their messenger boy and general flunky; but I stuck it out because being with them gave me greater prestige in my own age group. Besides fighting the usual gang wars and engaging in malicious mischief generally, we often branched out into various kinds of actually illegal endeavors. On one such occasion the older fellows used me to help them rob a nearby brewery: they hoisted me up to the second story of a barn-warehouse and I threw the goods down to them. A neighbor kid, who was jealous of all the extra prestige I was gaining, tipped off the police. They took me, a vile-screaming ten-year-old, to Juvenile Hall ("Juvy," we called it). Although what I had helped to steal was worth a substantial sum, the judge took pity on me and put me on probation, in the custody of my mother. Having two younger sons to look after as well, my mother was not a very good probation risk; although I never had any more run-ins with the police, my delinquency continued much as before.

Then Dad came home, a bitter and disillusioned man, and we moved to a smaller town. Of my three closest buddies in the gang that I left behind, two are now in prison and the other is a midshipman at Annapolis. Once settled in the new environment, I began to walk the straight and narrow. This was partly due to my father's harsher disciplinary methods, and partly to the fact that the new small-town environment simply wasn't conducive to delinquency. Although I hate to sound corny, what actually helped me most, in channelling my energies more constructively, was the fact that I became a member of the Boy Scouts. I also found, for the first time, that school work could be interesting. I began to do so well at it, in fact, that the principal wanted to move me up two grades, but my parents wisely refused to consent to this.

We didn't have much money, so when I was twelve years old my father told me that thenceforth I'd have to earn my own spending and clothes money. From that time on most of my free hours were taken up by a paper route and after-school odd jobs. I managed to earn enough even to be able to pay my parents a nominal fee of ten dollars a month for room and board. This early lesson in self-sufficiency was a great boon to me. Largely because of it, I quickly came to feel—as I do now in facing the prospect of college graduation —that I can come to grips with any situation I may encounter, and that I can do it without depending on anyone but myself.

Then we made another move. The reason—and not for the first time—was my father's relentless search for a job to satiate his desire for success and security (a desire, I might add, that was, and continues to be, frustrated at every turn). This time we lived in a large city, and I was able to make friends very easily through the Boy Scouts. I also continued to do well at school. I was elected president of my class, appointed Mayor for a Day in the annual Scout ceremonies, and soon felt that I was sitting on top of the world. But then we moved again, this time out to California.

The California environment was really new and strange. I couldn't even talk the same language as the kids my age. As far as they were concerned, I was a "square." In reaction, I became more and more of an introvert. To make matters worse, I began to grow; but I didn't stop growing like the other kids. Soon I was the tallest, clumsiest boy in the school. As I became the butt of everybody's jokes, I withdrew even further. After school I'd go straight home (home at the time was a trailer house) and sit in a corner drawing pictures, listening to the radio, and dreaming of becoming a commercial artist.

After a while, as my physique began to fill out and I learned again to co-ordinate, I gradually re-emerged from my shell. I discovered my forte on the basketball court; with my height, nobody else could stop my shots. All the next summer, after work, I practiced the game faithfully. With the first game of my sophomore year I was taken on the team. When, in that first game, I broke the scoring record, the whole world suddenly took on a different hue (even though I never did quite as well in any of the succeeding games).

I discovered that there was an opposite sex, and found

that I could speak the right language after all. But in the large, mushrooming cities of California, the environment is actually conducive to juvenile delinquency. In small part, I suppose, this is due to the proximity of an immoral Hollywood atmosphere. Mostly, however, it results from the fact that hundreds of new families are moving into these areas every day, and that their way of life is inevitably makeshift and temporary. Kids are unsettled and maladjusted; that is why they so easily follow the cult and ape the mannerisms of such screen stars as the late James Dean. During my own high-school days, our hero was Marlon Brando; we talked like him, walked like him, and imitated his every action. In the course of a summer laboring job, I fell in with a typical "fast crowd." I took to racing around on motorcycles and in souped-up hot rods, drank, smoked, and raised hell in general. What saved me from becoming a complete delinquent was the fact that I had, at the same time, become more and more interested in my studies. My grades were high; I found that I was a good debater; I was a member of the student council and editor of the high-school newspaper; and all in all, I was what we called a genuine BMOC (Big Man On Campus). I no longer needed the bravado of membership and prominence in a juvenile gang.

I never thought much about college, but was unexpectedly accepted and given a large scholarship by Princeton. I had never heard of the place, but had applied and taken the college entrance examinations at the urging of a friend of my father's who was an alumnus. It was the only college I applied to. When I came East for the first time in my life, I encountered education in the true sense of the word, as I had never known it before. I had to learn to think and write all over again. Once again I found myself in a totally new environment in which I couldn't speak the language. And what made it even more difficult was that everyone of my Princeton classmates were also ex-BMOC's. There was a new suaveness, a new vocabulary, a new style of dress; this was another situation for the survival of the fittest. Only this time I was not the smartest. And in fighting this new kind of battle—a battle of wits for prestige and honor—I had absolutely no previous experience.

I was soon very frustrated. I just couldn't make a name for myself, either in studies, sports, or extracurricular activities. For every failure I would have a logical excuse, a rationalization; it isn't easy to admit that you're just a little frog lost in an ocean. At first, as did the others in my situation, I withdrew and sulked. Then I tried something else. I began to shoot the bull, to try to impress my classmates with how important I was by bluffing them with big-talk stories about myself. But again the others were too smart for me. They listened politely enough, but then they excused themselves and left me alone.

But I had to do *something* to gain back the kind of attention I had once enjoyed. So instead of just talking big, I began to *act* big. For the third time in my life, I found myself resorting to delinquency: I started to drink heavily, to associate with whatever other "tough guys" I could find, and to embark on different kinds of grandiose and more or less "shady" business adventures. Although—as a by-product—I made considerable money at some of the business deals I concocted, I found, gradually, that my classmates were getting to like and respect me not *because* of my big acts, but *in spite* of them. Slowly I felt myself relaxing, saw my grades improving, and came to the conclusion, albeit an uncertain one, that maybe I could get along even *without* being a BMOC.

But the adjustment hasn't been easy. My Princeton experience has given me, I'm convinced, as fine an education as a man can get; yet in another sense it has left its scars and a lingering feeling of resentment. My first three years were miserable years of conforming when I didn't have enough money to conform. I felt rejected and frustrated and came to dislike not only the clothes, values and manners of the Ivy League, but the entire East in general. It was not until my last year at Princeton that I really became myself again: I wore boots to Junior Prom; refused to wear a tie, no matter how formal the occasion; and looked for genuine people who seemed to like me for what I was. This new approach has worked very well. As a result, the frustrations which hounded me for so long have gradually left me, and I have come to enjoy the University and its facilities to a much greater extent than I ever did before.

Now I am about to graduate. With all my rejection of so much of campus life, the whole experience has taught me something very important. From it, I have learned that the hard, competitive world which I shall face after graduation is nothing but an enlarged version of the situation I have already encountered and learned to cope with at college. In life at large, I will simply continue to treat every situation as one in which only the fittest will survive—exactly as I have had to do as a student. In order to make sure that *I* will be one of those fittest, and that I may achieve something in life, I'll have to act strictly in my own self-interest and on my own behalf. I expect a great deal out of life. Frankly, I even want to be famous. (If this chapter were not anonymous I would never have consented to write it, for it contains many statements and admissions that could seriously hinder me in my progress.)

I do not pretend to have any high ideal that guides me or that could serve to disguise my desire to achieve something and to be a success. On the contrary, everything I do is calculated—or at least intended—in some way to enhance my own position. I believe in taking the calculated risks, and no one is going to stop me. This does not mean that the only reason I have friends is to "use" them. Nor does it mean that my heart is untouchable. I simply believe that it's necessary to keep my private and my public lives separate enough so that they won't interfere with each other. As far as my public life goes, my hopes for the future are based on the assumption that I am going to have to take every short cut, every means at my disposal, to achieve my desired ends.

As yet I am undecided as to what these ends should be. I shall probably end up by going into business or law. What I know for certain is that the vocation I finally end up in will be one where I am my own boss. I can see myself working for a large corporation while I'm still shopping around for a field of endeavor to specialize in; but I could never become just one more member of society's millions of white-collar workers. It's much too easy to fall into a rut from which it is difficult, if not impossible, to escape. I know: I've seen my father in that same situation, and I've seen him try to compensate for his frustrations by taking it out on his sons. Furthermore, unlike so many of my classmates, I don't believe that the day of the individual entrepreneur is gone by any means. There are still plenty of opportunities for young men willing to take the calculated risks: such fields as real-estate development in California and Texas, and the exploitation of "new material" industries like Fiberglas, for example, are still wide open. There are also new and expanding opportunities in law that an aggressive young lawyer could get into, in the new field of labor law, for example. As an independent businessman or lawyer, I would feel most challenged and could use my philosophy of getting ahead in the world with the least possible outside interference. It occurs to me that a sociologist I know would call my seemingly ideal-less desire to get ahead at any price a case of the social disease of "anomie." Myself, I call it common sense.

I feel that law would be a good background for almost any field of enterprise I may decide upon. Certainly higher education of some type is just about a necessity if one is planning to make one's own "breaks" in life. So what I am most probably going to do is to put in another three years at law school. Before I do, however, I'm going to have to work for a year or two to earn the necessary money. When I tell people this, they ask, "But what about the draft?" To answer that question I have to be very blunt: the army represents everything that I can't stand. It is at once a prison, a policeman, a rut, and a control. If I went into the service I'd be a slave, I wouldn't be my own boss, I'd have to obey people so stupid that I'd ordinarily have nothing to do with them. So, barring a war situation, in which I'd probably volunteer, I'm going to do my utmost to avoid having to go into the service. How? By educating myself out of it, by going to school until I'm too old to be drafted. It'll be nip and tuck, but I think I can make it.

By this point the reader may be inclined to write off my plans for life as unrealistic, on the assumption that one of these days I'll get married, settle down to a nice, steady corporation job, and raise so many children that I won't be able to afford to chance the calculated risks I've talked about. However, my views of marriage are very radical and, I believe, fit in very well with my other plans. I believe that marriage is a mutual project in which the husband and his wife form a team working together for success. Sure, I'll marry for love (whatever that may be), but I'm going to insist that when I do take a wife she be strictly a career woman. She cannot be a homebody who wants a little bungalow in which to raise a large family. I don't want a family. I want freedom. I want to be able to take the calculated risks to get ahead quickly; I don't want the responsibility of having to protect a dependent wife or innocent children if my calculated risks should misfire. Whatever vocation I choose, I'll probably be having to spend a good many days away from home, and I don't want any kids of mine to be brought up in the sort of fatherless atmosphere that I myself experienced for three years. Of course, if I should marry and should somehow slip up, in that case I'll just have to make the best of it and react like any other normal, decent father.

What I have to do is to find a girl who is compatible and who either doesn't want children or, better still, is unable to have them.

Needless to say, these views of mine on marriage have made my dating experiences pretty miserable at times. Women are such predatory creatures. They are always anxious to get married as fast as possible and to raise a flock of kids. And they're often not very subtle in showing their desires. As a result, my typical dating sequence has been something like this: I take the girl out and we find that we have much in common and are very compatible; we go out on two or three further dates and find we are becoming very fond of each other; she sweetly takes me window-shopping for engagement rings, bedroom sets, and bassinets; and thereafter I do not go out on a date with her again. I've been engaged twice, and each time it has been this desire of the girl in question for a family right away which has caused me to become disengaged again.

As far as my morals on the subject of sex go, I think my attitudes are fairly ordinary. I believe in necking, petting, and so on, but after a while, I find, that gets boring, and then I want a girl with whom I can talk intelligently. I used to believe that I should try to "go all the way" with every girl I took out, but I have learned from experience that that is not a wise thing to do. One of the girls to whom I was engaged lived with me for a month as though we were actually married. We didn't believe that we were doing anything immoral; we were just testing our compatibility. Our actions backfired on us— or so we thought—when she missed her period twice in a row and I, in my concern for her and myself, came close to flunking out of school. Luckily it proved a false alarm, but I adjusted my way of thinking fast. Now I never try to go all the way with a girl; in fact, I no longer let myself get into the kind of situations where I might even be tempted. This is not a matter of morality, of course. The point is simply that I don't want to get involved in anything that would reflect on my character in the future, and that I don't want to find myself married and with family even before I get started in a career.

My views on religion have been another matter that has complicated my relations with girls. My theory of religion is very liberal. Basically, I do not believe in any particular church, and I do not have faith in Christ; I do, however, believe in God. I was baptized and brought up in the Methodist Church and have experimented with Catholicism, Quakerism, Unitarianism, and Christian Science. What turns me away from all kinds of organized religion is, above all, the ceremony and ritual that they involve. In fact, the only religion that really appeals to me is one that was developed by an ex-master sergeant and, from what I read somewhere, has been called the GI religion. The services of this religion are modeled after those which were used in the bunkers of World War II and the Korean War just before the men went into battle and when there were no chaplains available. You simply walk into a dark room, sit, stand, or kneel—as you prefer, and worship your own God (or whatever you choose to call Him), in your own personal way: no music, no sermon, no vocal prayers— everything strictly spontaneous. That encompasses just about my ideal of what religion should be.

As far as my philosophy of life goes, religion plays almost no part at all. As a matter of fact, there is actually only one determining consideration in my philosophy—me and my desire to survive on the terms that I may set for myself. This means that I worry very little about abstractions. In fact, writing this chapter has been the first time that I've tried really to be introspective. Normally, when I think or do something, I never ask myself the reason. When I have thought or acted in some way, I simply assume that somehow I did so, even though unconsciously, because I figured it was good for me. If some of my friends turn against me for an action, I find that they have soon forgotten about it. And in the long run, somehow, most of the actions I take do work out for my benefit.

Many of my friends worry a lot about making decisions. When they face a situation, they stop to weigh the pros and cons before deciding what course to take. This is something I do very seldom. I just act. What the consequences are I think about later. This, of course, leads to many seemingly crazy actions on my part. For example, often in college I have gotten the feeling that I want to go somewhere, anywhere, and I've found someone crazy enough to go with me. One winter, a friend and myself would go out to the nearest highway, where he would get on one side of the road, and I would stand on the other side. We would put our thumbs out, and the first one to get a ride would call the other over. Then we'd ride and hitchhike as far in that direction as we could get by morning. I believe this tendency to act without any thought is a carry-over from the days when my survival depended upon my ability to make quick decisions. The self-sufficiency forced upon me by my father, and the necessity of having had to survive in situations where you'd get kicked even if you were down, are the two main causes, I believe, which have produced my whole egocentric philosophy of life. My parents have always told me that I was too egotistical. So have the girls I've known. I agree. I am egotistical. But the reason, quite simply, is that I'm convinced that if you want to get anywhere in this world of dog-eat-dog, you *have* to be egotistical. I once ran across a paraphrase of the Biblical Golden Rule: Do unto others as they would do unto you, but do it first. That's my motto.

I'd like, at this point, to make a little confession. I think that I should admit that there are some occasional lapses in my neatly laid-out ideas, ideals, likes, and dislikes. Sometimes I stop and think that I really don't want to be famous at all. I sometimes wish that I could have faith in a simple, standard religion. At times I find myself dreaming about how nice it would be just to get married, settle down, raise a couple of kids, and spend Saturday mornings clipping my front lawn. There have been times, even, when I've thought it would be fun to walk into a recruiting center, enlist, and just become a truck driver in the Transportation Corps. And at other times still, in a slightly different mood, I've felt like committing a perfect bank robbery, buying a truckload of books and classical records, and retiring to a mythical hideout in the mountains of western Colorado (where I was once deer hunting).

But these doubts are only an undercurrent. For all practical purposes, I hold to my original thoughts and plans. But often, when I think about the avenues I will have to travel to become a success, I wonder whether the future will be such that anyone in America will be *able* to advance to prestige or power. How long will there *be* an America as we know it today? Where is this teeming, explosive bi-polar world going? Will the power struggle between the United States and Russia ultimately end in a global war? I like to hope that peace will eventually come, but underneath I'm very much afraid that it won't.

As I see it, there are now two dominant "religions" in the world ("dominant" in the sense that they are identified with the world's two greatest powers). One is Christianity and the other is communism. America is founded on basic Christian precepts, but it seems to me that Americans are no longer willing to risk their lives for what their country stands for. I wonder how many Americans in Korea really knew what they were fighting for and felt any strong emotion about it? The vast majority, I would guess, went into the armed forces because they were drafted, and fought simply because they had to as part of their units. Their fighting spirit was mostly a matter of crowd psychology.

The Communists, on the other hand—like the Christians in Ancient Rome—believe fanatically in their religion, and they are dying for it every day. Partly because of the compelling example of this fanaticism, the Communist religion is advancing in underdeveloped and insecure areas everywhere. Granted, many of the Communist leaders are simply power-hungry opportunists; but the rank and file, I am afraid, are terrifyingly sincere. And with us, in contrast—well, there seems to me to be no better example of our timidity than our reaction to the recent attempted revolution in Hungary, in October, 1956. The government responded with heroic help-lessness, the people with sentimental apathy, and nowhere was there a real fighting concern for the defense of what America stands for. Yet unless we are willing to die for the survival of freedom and the Christian precepts upon which our nation was built, we are doomed. It will only be a question of time. I for my part *am* willing to risk my life for my country. But the reason I am prepared to do this is not, I must admit, a matter of pure patriotism. It is, rather, the conviction that the realization of the future I have mapped out for myself depends upon the existence of a free, capitalistic and liberal democratic America. I would fight for my country because in doing so I would be fighting for my own fulfillment.

This, in brief, is me and my thoughts as best I can put them down. As I have said, I am not very good at this business of introspection. What the fulfillment I have spoken of may consist of, I don't know. All I *do* know is that I'm confident that whatever situations may come up, I'll be ready. I shall take the calculated risks, and hope that they will produce the kind of results which will bring me the satisfaction of having accomplished something in life. What that something may turn out to be, I can only guess.

TO DECIDE FOR ONESELF

To BEGIN WITH, I SUPPOSE, I should say that my values and aspirations are conditioned by a feeling of great inexperience. My life has been neither very interesting nor at all unusual. I have never faced any grave responsibilities, difficult situations, or troubling moral decisions. Whether this fact has kept me a little immature, I cannot really tell; I feel that it undoubtedly must somewhat affect my viewpoint. Now that I am graduating from college, to be forced at last to do a little independent thinking and acting, it is perhaps a good idea to take stock for a moment of the values which I have derived from my upbringing and education.

Typical of my life is the fact that my family has done very little moving around. Born and raised in New York City, I have never, except on Naval ROTC summer cruises, been outside of the continental United States or, for that matter, west of the east coastal states. I shall have occasion to mention my parents frequently in this discussion, because their influence has been very great in my life. Not only have I been around my parents almost constantly, but in addition, both of them have taken a very close and detailed interest in my life and activities.

My mother spent her girlhood in New Jersey and, after graduating from college, obtained a job in Manhattan during the 1930's. She came from a large family, and her mother was one of those remarkable, strong personalities that one sometimes meets. The old lady made quite an impression on her kids, Mother especially. Sometimes I think she scared them to death, but whatever her technique, she brought them up to be unselfish and to love and be interested in other people. It sounds corny, but that's the way that family was taught to act. All her life, as a result, the most important thing for my mother has been what one might call "human relations." Every experience she is inclined to evaluate, therefore, in terms of making friends, and every moral decision in terms of how others will be affected. This attitude is by no means restricted to the immediate family, but is directed towards everybody. Needless to say, my mother's gift for making friends has been of great value to our family, especially since the rest of us are not by nature the best mixers. There is, however, one major drawback to my mother's family, with their tradition of living by the Golden Rule in mass fashion. In the name of love, friendliness, unselfishness, etc., they have a tendency to pry into each other's affairs and those of other persons (myself, for instance) who resent having to account for every moment of their time to some doting aunt. Nevertheless, this is a small gripe, and as it is my firm intention to have considerably less to do with my family in the future than I have had in the past, I shall not bother myself much, henceforth, on the matter of curious relatives.

While I owe my mother a great deal in terms of the social side of my upbringing and family life, I feel much closer to my father. He and I have had very different childhoods, with the result that we have discovered many of our basic values to be poles apart. He still, I think, has some strong misconceptions about the fundamental premises which I act upon, and will probably never understand me fully because I am of a different generation. But I at least now understand his motivations pretty well, so that the great misunderstandings of my earlier years will probably not be repeated. My father and I are very similar in temperament and personality, and I somehow think of him as a stronger character and more substantial person than my mother. These, I guess, are the reasons for my greater respect and feeling for him. For all our different values, we seem to have the same sort of systematic approach to our problems.

There are several reasons why I shall dwell at some length upon my father's background and outlook on life. For one thing, my father's ideas and attitudes have had a strong impact upon me, and in order to know myself I have been obliged to put my father's influence in its proper perspective. Then, too, as I have already pointed out, I have felt very close to my father, but have taken a long time to understand him. Gaining this understanding has necessarily included a certain degree of self-examination and has been an important problem in my life.

Dad's father died when Dad was not yet eight years of age. His mother and her brothers consequently bore the brunt of his education and upbringing. From the time of my grand-father's death, my father was carefully taught two major principles: first, that he was head of the family and would have to be prepared to do much of the thinking and decision-making for it; and second, since my grandfather's death had left the family without much money, that he would have to be prepared to make whatever sacrifices might be necessary to support it. All his life, therefore, he has been making sacrifices, first for his mother and brother, then for his wife and children. Most fathers must do this, but few have done so to the extent that Dad has. Born in the South, he came to New York to enter business after graduating from college, giving up the hope of graduate school so that his brother could utilize the modest family funds for this purpose. He works, like many business-men, in a fierce, uncompromising way, with rare vacations. But he does so not so much because business has become his life, as with some men, but simply because it is the family's only source of income and because he is a perfectionist who has always believed that nothing should be undertaken without putting maximum effort into it. My father, I honestly think, knows little happiness besides the satisfaction of a job well done. He cannot understand, or at least cannot condone, anyone who does something purely for pleasure, amusement, or recreation. I don't know when he has ever used the word "fun." In short, there are two precepts which might be called my father's fundamental values. Both may be described by clichés which I shall use for the sake of brevity. The first is that what is worth doing is worth doing well; the second (paraphrasing the Biblical quotation) is that you should do your best in that state of life to which it has pleased God to call you.

I disagree with both of my father's main values. There are things, I have found, which are of value and are worth doing, but which are hardly so important as to justify a maximum effort. My Navy work on summer cruises and in college constitutes an example: I can do a better than average job with moderate effort, whereas a great deal more effort would only produce moderate improvement. I prefer to judge what things are of the greatest value and to apportion my effort accordingly. Some things, in other words, are more "worth doing" than others and therefore require and deserve more effort.

Similarly, I resist my father's second value—acceptance of one's lot in life. There are people, attitudes, and institutions around me about which I have developed strong opinions. There are those things which need change, abolition, or revision; there are others in the process of change or decay which I would preserve. You can experience a healthy dissatisfaction with the world and your place in it without becoming a frustrated neurotic. Certainly, acceptance of an unavoidable situation is an important quality. But I will not be told to pattern myself entirely according to the apparent dictates of the world. I've been told a thousand times that I can't change the world to suit myself, but I will not admit it. Thousands may have struggled vainly against the world and society, and died unhappy because of it. But man has no hope if he doesn't keep on trying to correct what he feels to be wrong. Maybe, in a few years, I shall become a happy, relatively conforming family man who has no desire to change things. But now, at the age of twenty-one, I cannot resign myself to the *principle* of acceptance which my father preaches. Granted, the era of the Big Solution, if it ever existed, is past now, and only painstaking, piecemeal efforts can hope for success in solving society's problems. But such efforts must be made as long as there can be found people with youth, energy, brains, and ideas. Only a dynamic society survives, and only the relentless efforts of those who form opinions and do not simply adjust to the ideas and expectations of others make possible such a dynamism. More than anything else, it has been the contact with thinking people afforded by a Princeton education which has caused my rejection of the two basic values of my father. I shall now try to explain how my current efforts to balance properly the values of my parents and those of my education came about.

My father had been in business a good many years before he married Mother, with the result that he had a fairly good salary. And although this has been our only source of income, we have been able to live rather comfortably and would probably be fairly well-to-do in a less expensive community than New York City. Of course, there have been no frills (as I said, we have done no travelling), but I certainly have no complaints as to financial status. I have never been to a public or coeducational school. After my primary schooling in Manhattan, I went South to prep school for four years and then to Princeton. Until I was about eleven years old, I hated exercise and athletics, and ducked any activity requiring physical or manual skill whenever I could. There were, I think, several reasons for this. First of all, I was an excellent student but physically small for my age; so I quite naturally turned to those things at which I could most easily excel. But the main reason for the dislike of athletics and my tendency to be an introvert until I went away to school was my father's attitude towards sports. Recognizing the desirability of being a good mixer and of having at least some athletic ability, my father always encouraged me to participate in group activities and in sports. Unfortunately, however, he never suggested that such activities might be fun or enjoyable for their own sake. "Constructive" was the word he always used, and as long as I live that word will haunt me. I was constantly urged to "improve" myself, which, as far as I was concerned, had the effect of placing activities pursued by most children for recreation and pleasure on a par with eating spinach. From my earliest days, doing what was constructive or designed to improve me was associated in my mind with unpleasantness or punishment. My poor father struggled for years to make a baseball player out of me. When I went to prep school and became an almost fanatical baseball enthusiast on my own, I regretted that my failure to enjoy the game while I was younger had had the effect of so badly retarding me as an athlete.

I did not like New York at all during my early years, probably because my distaste for athletics and other group activities made me an introvert. Manhattan is not a good place for young people anyway, since there is relatively little of that natural and spontaneous neighborhood social fun among kids which is so important a part of life in smaller communities.

When I went away to prep school in 1949, I was even more naïve and sheltered than that traditionally comic character, the new arrival at boarding school. In accordance with parental admonitions, I worked very hard when I first arrived, but I soon found that I had been so well prepared that the work came very easily. For the next two years, therefore, I managed, with a minimum of work, to stay near the top of my class and was left plenty of time for the normal gamut of prep-school escapades. Group endeavors at prep school were for the most part anything but constructive, and as a result I found them most enjoyable.

In addition to the sundry escapades we had at prep school and some of the characters who were our teachers, I shall most of all never forget the boys themselves. In the last ten years, I have come to know well a large number of Southerners, and I feel that several generalities may be made concerning them. Their attitudes about current issues, foreign and domestic, to the extent that they have such attitudes, are positively archaic; reactionary is too mild a word. They are, however, as modern as one can possibly be when it comes to owning the latest appliances (especially cars) and going to the latest and fanciest places. They also tend to be much more prejudiced about minorities (and I don't mean just Negroes) than those of us from the Manhattan melting pot. But as people with whom to associate socially, they are absolutely without peer. The old hospitality gag is no lie. The Southerners I have met, whether in school, college, the Navy, or elsewhere, are gracious as hosts and sincerely friendly, even to strangers. They are superb party-givers and seem to lack the provincialism I tend to attribute to many Midwesterners.

The last two years of my sojourn in boarding school were spent largely at that frenzied participation in extracurricular activities which used to be an essential for admission to college in the days before Princeton started concentrating on unsociable mental giants and technical students. In due course I was admitted to college under the Navy program and came to Princeton, rooming at first with two former prep-school friends.

The first two years at Old Nassau were from a social standpoint rather barren except, of course, for a number of New York debutante parties during the Christmas vacations. My friends at college were not numerous, and we did not have too many parties, though we were conscientious moviegoers. Like many other Princetonians, I had edited a school paper and so, when the Press Club elections came around, was tempted by visions of journalistic fame. I decided against this potentially lucrative activity, however, because I feared that it would consume too much time. Shunning also the celebrated *Daily Princetonian,* I settled for a less important but more competently prepared publication which required a minimum of time, enabled me to make both friends and money, and gave me a chance to feel like a "doer" of sorts. For the most part, freshman and sophomore years were years in which I tried to "take advantage" of college. I knew I would eventually major in history. I was weak in such things as literature and art and loathed science and mathematics, although I had always done well at them. That left me a social science, and history had always been my favorite. I could remember names, dates, and obscure genealogical data almost photographically; and since I could also read fast, the history department seemed a natural. Being saddled with an uninspiring and academically worthless Naval Science class each term, I had to be careful in selecting courses if I were to get much out of college. And I can say with some pride that I never took a course that did not teach me a good deal. I had my share of "gut" courses, it is true, but I never selected them for their easiness, and I attended them conscientiously. These first two years were my conscientious years (I still avoid the word "constructive") and in them I gained that important academic experience at which the liberal university aims—the realization that there are many different viewpoints and many different approaches to human problems, and that no set of values or ideas need be the only "true" one.

Before passing to the glorious and irresponsible pleasures of my final two years, I should remark upon another most important phase of my education, namely, three Naval ROTC

summer cruises in which I participated and which, if nothing else, had a very favorable effect in broadening my outlook. Prep school and college never seemed to be so much of an experience of being "away from home" as were those eight weeks on a destroyer in the Atlantic in 1954. I always got nervous in the Navy uniform. It seemed as if there were a million customs, regulations, etc., that I was bound to violate through ignorance or ineptitude, and I always felt as if every person in the Navy were personally scrutinizing me and waiting to turn me in for some minor transgression. The military man has always been a source of wonder to me anyway. On my ship that first summer, the competent officers were "short-timers," and the career men all struck me as small-minded dullards who had little personality, seemed dreadfully conformist and unimaginative, and, above all, showed that distorted perspective which considers trivial deviations from routine as crises and neglects the matters which really are important. Among the enlisted men, strangely, it was often the other way around, with the senior petty officers being men of real ability and the one-enlistment men generally impressing me as the closest thing to the scum of society that I had as yet observed. I was the only third classman from Princeton on that ship, and aside from a handful of excellent men from Dartmouth and Virginia, the midshipmen were almost all from the universities in the so-called Big Ten. There were many aspects of that cruise that I at first hated: my initial seasickness; the hot, smelly and crowded living compartments (now quite familiar but then a horrible new experience); the incredibly bad food; and the tedium of countermanded orders and irrational changes in "the word." But all those objections were overcome by time, as I realized that they are merely inevitable characteristics of a military organization. The one aspect of that cruise that made me the most miserable, however, was the nature of my fellow midshipmen. With their coeducational colleges and national fraternities, not to mention the fact that they were almost all engineers, they lived in a different world from me. I made things worse through a kind of outspoken, aggressive loudness which did not win for me many friends. In short, I found these hulking denizens of our proudest state universities to be narrow-minded, humorless, unreasonably contemptuous of Ivy Leaguers, incapable of deep thought, and above all boring. Had they not been bores I could have tolerated all the rest. When we arrived in Cuba and had shore liberty, nearly all of them were blind drunk after the second Budweiser, thereby bringing my opinion of their capabilities to a suitable culmination. Now, after three cruises, however, I can say that I have grown to find these persons more cosmopolitan and personally less dull, while I have become more tolerant and less offensively outspoken. It seems strange that one must learn to get along with fellow Americans, but that was my problem, and the Navy cruises gave me an essential experience in human relations that I had never needed or gained in prep school or college.

It was really my second cruise, which followed sophomore year, that launched my "social" period at Princeton. For one thing, it was not a cruise at all, but was a six-week training period spent at two naval bases in the States, where we studied respectively amphibious war and principles of aviation. It was something of a ball after the preceding summer. The material they taught us was the most interesting and the best presented of any instruction I have received from the Navy up to this time. There were few watches to stand, shorter working hours, more chance for liberty, and opportunities to use Officer's Club and beach facilities. Above all, the thirty-odd members of the Princeton unit lived together, and I was able to make some close college friends whom otherwise I might never have gotten to know. After a summer of fairly social activities with these other Princetonians, it was easy to continue in the same vein on my return to college. Also, I guess, I was by then more sure of myself than I had ever been before. Not only did I have a high academic average, but I was safely in an eating club, "just above the middle" in social standing (most Princetonians feel that their club is just above the middle), was editor of a college publication, and even could hold my own in the intramural sports we played during that summer.

Back at Princeton, I was rooming with eight of my new clubmates, most of whom I barely knew. It soon developed that the club as a whole looked upon our rooms as the center of impromptu parties on campus, and as we occupied three living rooms, there was room enough for studying as well as social life. Although my work, both academic and extracurricular, was the most difficult of my life during junior year, my average was the highest that I ever attained.

Senior year proved to be much of a repetition of junior year, except that I had considerably less academic work and that the drinking, while I engaged in it more often, had lost some of its appeal. The weekends, however, continued to be wild and enjoyable. My dates were generally girls who liked gay parties, and I imagine that I shall miss those party weekends more than anything else.

In my senior year, also, I had an experience which has made me think a great deal about Princeton, people, and the values people use in judging one another. When the Bicker, or rushing, came along in December, I was the Bicker chairman for my club, following on the heels of a friend of mine who had done a particularly fine job in this capacity the year before. The class of 1959 at Princeton, which we were considering in the club elections, had the distinction, I understand, of having more Jews in it and proportionately fewer prep-school graduates than any other class in Princeton's history. While I do have a distinct preference for prep-school graduates, many of my friends are not from prep school and I am not strongly opinionated on the subject. Similarly, I have many Jewish friends and am not personally prejudiced against Jews except in the realm of international politics. But as club Bicker chairman I was faced with a deplorable situation. According to Princeton's social standards, there were appallingly few "good men" available. The "name" of one's club depends in large measure upon the number of prep-school graduates and tweed-clad extroverts that are among its members. The Princeton club is primarily for the social side of life. There is no room for the nondrinker, the silent introvert, or the man who spends so much time on studies that he neglects the social life which is so much a part of college. Whatever my personal prejudice, or lack of it, I had to resist the admission to the club of those types who by the accepted, traditional standards were not suitable for a social organization. Such persons were generally brilliant high-school graduates who had to combat the handicap of inadequate secondary-school preparation by concentrating on academic work to the exclusion of most other pursuits. Even the so-called prejudice against Jews, I found, was not so much an opposition to them as such, as to the fact that most of them (either because they were "grinds" or because they felt ill at ease among prep-school socialites) were simply poor mixers and did not fit well into a purely social organization.

Because Bicker is for two short weeks a really earth-shaking experience for most of the Princetonians involved, I have discussed the problems it raises at some length. For the first time I realized the very real conflict between the social and academic side of life in college. A Princeton education, in terms of its content and outlook, is perhaps the best college education obtainable in America. My first two years of college, in which I had emphasized the intellectual side of life, had been really rewarding. Yet I knew that, like thousands of Princetonians before me, I would love Princeton not primarily for the academic education, but for my club and my social life. It would be a recollection of good friends and good times that would induce me in later years to give money to Princeton. However

I might look back on rewarding academic work, this would always seem secondary. My senior thesis I did not start until February. But once I got started on it, I worked very hard and, despite its inadequacies, I feel it was well written and deserved the relatively high grade it received. My future will be in the academic profession, for I have for a long time had the ambition to teach history on the college level. I mention these facts now to show that I did not go to college just for kicks. When I say that I shall remember Princeton most affectionately for the social side of life there, I say so as a person who has taken and will continue to take academic work very seriously.

I believe, in addition, that the slogan "Princeton in the nation's service" is a very meaningful one. But I think that the ideal implied may quite possibly be fulfilled best by the man whose abilities definitely include a proper training in the social graces. I believe that a person graduating from Princeton with an average mark is probably better educated academically than are many honors graduates from other colleges. Princeton's primary function, I believe, as is that of most of the Ivy League schools, is to maintain an honorable tradition of supplying the nation with men whose intelligence and breadth of outlook are coupled with a capacity for dealing easily with others. Princeton should not be in business to develop technicians. It is possible, I feel, that the club system, whatever its inherent evils, has a greater place at Princeton than the brilliant but colorless and socially ill-at-ease individual who spends his four college years closeted in a library or laboratory. It may sound snobbish to say it, but I think the university should remember the types who have given it not only its support but also its honored name. To me, the "country club" appellation sometimes flung at Princeton is no more than the envious viciousness of the socially self-conscious individual who resents the idea that you can be superbly educated and have fun with your friends at the same time. This impression derived from my senior year and from my experience with

Princeton's Bicker system is perhaps the last great lesson I have acquired from college.

Now that I am about to become a naval officer for three years, I feel that my biggest immediate problem will be the assumption of responsibility. My life has been so free of major adjustments, and my parents have been so solicitous of my welfare, that I have had few occasions or opportunities to make decisions. Since I have rather conservative plans for the future, perhaps these coming few years in the Navy will be my only great chance to grow up. After I have finished my Navy duty, I hope to go to graduate school and obtain a Ph.D. in history or some other branch of the social sciences. Being a college professor would give me an opportunity both to teach and to write. If, as time goes by, the writing side should interest me more, I shall turn to some more journalistic field of endeavor.

I have, quite naturally, a great desire ultimately to get married and raise four or five bright children. Somehow, I feel that I missed many things in my youth because of where I lived and the kinds of schools I went to. Up to this time I have made no mention of my relations with the other sex, mainly because I don't believe that these relations have had any effect to speak of in my development. I had an innocent but very pleasant love affair when I was sixteen, but after two months of going steady it came to nothing. Since then I have had my occasional crushes, but my girl friends have been on the whole a group of pleasant but rather shallow debutantes who have served as rather disinterested sexual partners or as drinking companions for college weekends and New York parties. Perhaps I shall grow more serious towards women when I have a few responsibilities and a little more money.

Although I think the family is very important, and long for the day when I shall have my own family, I feel very strongly at the present time the need to escape from my own parents. My brother once put it very aptly when he said that our family life at home has reached the point where one feels an almost constant atmosphere of parental disapproval. I have come to suspect very strongly, in fact, that the relations of parents and sons may be a very vital social problem for all America. Just as I now feel that I am subjected to too much family, many youngsters have doubtless suffered far greater ill effects from lack of parental attention. Parental upbringing should, as such, cease around the age of eighteen. If they haven't taught one the difference between right and wrong by that time, they never will. After the age of eighteen, parents are still important, as people who are sufficiently interested in you to listen to your problems sympathetically. I for one am sick of being told my obvious mistakes whenever I have gotten into some difficulty. I usually know what I did wrong. What I want now is to have somebody to tell me it's all right. Perhaps that's why I want to get married and have my own family. I see so many of my friends shunning their parents and taking their problems to sympathetic girl friends.

I have come to feel that many of our current values, aspirations, and frustrations seem to bear a relationship to our youth and family life. But as mutual understanding between parents and children has become more and more important in our current society, it has become much more complicated. The world, especially as seen from the vantage point of twentieth-century America, has, in the past fifty years, been changing in a revolutionary manner. Wars, depressions, ideologies, shifts in public opinion, and technological innovation have followed one another with greater rapidity and wider implications with each successive generation. My point, therefore, is this: basic values in the country are changing in such a way that there is a greater gap between the fundamental assumptions and aspirations of ourselves and those of our parents than there has been between the outlooks of any two successive generations in the past. For instance, my parents knew war in their youth, but in their college years the United States was busily and optimistically returning to "normalcy" and prosperity. There was no atomic bomb, no expectation of almost inevitable military service, no television; there were far fewer autos whereas they are now considered practically a necessity for one's social life even during the high-school and college years. With prohibition in force, liquor was not the major social prop it now is, at least in the colleges in the eastern United States. How different in their effect upon the thinking of American youth have been these changes, compared to the more gradual changes between my grandfather's youth and that of my father! How easy for any parent to forget this fact and to brand as wrong the things "not done in my day" instead of accepting them as inevitable, amoral changes in society which simply must be adjusted to!

The matter of religion is one which has concerned me a great deal in recent years. My mother and father being Episcopalians, I too was naturally brought up as one. But neither parent was very doctrinaire when it came to religious views. My father has always conducted himself with a certain ethical scrupulousness and has, on occasion, given vent to Biblical quotations. But these have been the only notable signs of religion that I have detected in him. He is, in short, a practicing Christian who has never been forced to develop any detailed articles of faith. For my mother, church attendance and a sort of Golden Rule morality have constituted her religion. Both parents, especially Mother, have expressed unhappiness when I have from time to time been critical of religious practice or expressed dogmatic views of my own.

I regard religion as a sort of emotional device whereby man seeks to understand a handful of basic questions about himself and his origin when man-made scientific theories and devices fail him. To me it is a serious error to equate morality with religion. Religion is a matter of personal faith, of belief in something unprovable. It may be used to help sanction one's personal moral code and to guide one's actions, but whereas there may be religious absolutes, albeit subjective ones, there cannot, at least as I see it, be any absolute or unchanging moral law. I believe in the absolute dignity and integrity of the human soul, and the capacity of every human being to establish his own values and standards. For instance, I do not believe there is inherently or absolutely anything wrong with pre-marital or extra-marital sexual intercourse. If somebody is hurt physically, morally, or spiritually by such an act, then it is wrong. But if there is no regret or remorse, only joy, there can be no immorality. My own few sexual experiences have been mainly physical. They have not been accompanied by any sublime feeling between the persons involved. On the other hand, there has been no remorse on either side, and there has consequently been no sin.

Because my own personal religion tends to be very utilitarian, I am quite naturally rather tolerant of, or should I say indifferent to, religious beliefs of others. I do, however, make one exception. That exception is the Roman Catholic religion, which I regard with disgust. To me it is a religion based entirely on fear, not the wholesome, inward fear of God described in the Bible, but a fear deliberately generated by a worldly institution with the apparent aims of raising money, of perpetuating itself, and of controlling the lives and minds of its credulous subjects. It is not, however, the religious doctrine of the Catholic Church, with its elaborate casuistry and ritual, which has caused me to take my extreme position against Catholicism. There are three other specific reasons why I have developed my viewpoint. First of all, as a history student studying the role of the Church and especially of the Jesuits since the later Middle Ages, I find that the record of these institutions makes them unworthy of respect. Secondly, I have noticed from my friends in business and society that Catholics exhibit clannishness, a tendency to associate with and promote the interests of fellow Catholics at the expense of more deserving persons of other religious persuasions. Finally, and above all, the Roman Catholic Church has been discredited completely in my eyes by the appalling conduct of a certain Catholic priest who, during my years at Princeton, has shown considerably more interest in the university's affairs than a good many people would think his office called for. Unable to restrain himself after having made a few valid criticisms of the scholarship of the Princeton religion department, this priest has attacked the whole concept of a liberal education in a most insulting manner. More serious still, he has displayed the most annoying and dangerous characteristic of the Catholic Church, namely, a type of meddling in political and cultural matters tantamount to demagoguery. Here is my greatest anxiety concerning the Catholic Church: a powerful international organization capitalizes upon the sacred religion of millions of persons and upon a very real fear of Communist terrorism, to promote its own brand of authoritarianism, intolerance and political reaction.

The criticisms of Princeton made by this priest I find so very important because they point up what I consider the most valuable part of a Princeton or liberal education. As I understand the critic, he assumes a basic degree of immaturity and inability to make decisions or to think deeply on the part of the college undergraduate; and acting on this assumption, he warns that a college must teach such people only what is "right," only "the truth." This attitude is the historic view of the Catholic Church and is a view which is held, I am afraid, by a good segment of the general population. It is, however, completely antithetical to the spirit of the liberal education at which Princeton purports to aim. I believe that the great value of Princeton from an academic standpoint is its effort to expose the student to all viewpoints, to release him from the inevitably narrow assumptions that govern the upbringing of most youngsters, and to let the individual, after he has tried to understand all the important motivations and values which men have held throughout history, search his soul and his experience for the values *he* shall adopt. This principle I believe to be the most enduring and valuable idea I have gained at Princeton. And as I seek to become a college professor in future years, it is my determination to adhere to the belief that each man must find his own truth after learning the realities and truths that exist for others; that each man, in other words, must decide for himself.

ARMY BRAT

IN LESS THAN A MONTH I will be graduating from college. During these last weeks the main topic of conversation among the liberal-arts majors has been, "What are you planning to do after June eighteenth?" I seem to be the only one who has replied that I have accepted a commission in the Regular Army and at present plan to make a career of the military.

To most people my decision to enter the military and my choice of Princeton as my alma mater just don't seem to jibe. Princeton and Princetonians are dead set against anything which even smells of the military. I generally explain my actions by telling people that my father is an officer in the army and that I chose Princeton only after my lifelong ambition to become a West Pointer was ended by poor eyesight. And at least the latter part of this explanation is true. When I received word that I had flunked the West Point physical, the entire complexion of my life changed. Until then my course had been laid out before me as plain as the handwriting on the wall. I was to have gone to the "Point," received my commission, married another army brat, and have spent the rest of my life as an army officer with an ever-growing family and the inevitable twenty-year mortgage. When the door to the Military Academy closed in my face, I was forced to come out of my shell and look at life and the part I could play in it. It was my first big step in the direction of becoming what I consider a genuine human being.

Perhaps a glance at my background will explain why I feel that until that day I had not really been an "individual." Born in a small town in western Pennsylvania, I was just a member of another small-town family, destined to grow up and probably die in that same small town. That was until my father accepted a second lieutenant's commission in the army in 1940. From that day on my life took on a new direction and I became one of those strange beings, an army brat.

My January birthdate and my well-above-average intelligence soon put me two years ahead of my age group in school. This age differential, more than any other single factor, has made me what I am. My inferior age and physical size left me outside of the groups formed by my classmates in grade school and forced me to fall back upon my own resources and the companionship of my younger brother and his friends. I began to associate with these younger children because it gave me a position of superiority which I so dearly missed in my dealings with my classmates. This need for feeling equal or superior to my classmates and all people in general is the primary drive which has led me to the acceptance of a military career. It led me to attend a military high school for two years. When I became a company commander senior year I reached the peak of my struggle for equality. My stock answer, therefore, referring to my father's military career, really has no validity at all. I use it merely as an unembarrassing way to satisfy the general public. Actually, my father is the most unmilitary man ever to grace an army uniform. Don't misunderstand me, he is a wonderful officer. His seventeen-year career as a reserve officer will attest to that. He is, however, only an officer because his fling at being a general contractor failed financially. At heart he remains a contractor rather than a lieutenant colonel in the army. And Mother is the same way. She hates to move and has grown to dislike the army because for months at a time it has taken away her husband and is soon also to take her eldest son. Her world consists of our family.

The army has fed that world, but it has also pushed it around
and, at times, broken it up. As you might expect, therefore, my
choice of a military career has not been encouraged by either
of my parents. They have gone along with it only because it
has been my wish. And Dad, of course, has been a big help by
pulling a few strings and checking into whatever problems
have faced me.

I would like to be able to say that I have decided on the
military as a career because I feel that this country needs a
more competent officer corps or because I get a lump in my
throat every time someone speaks of the Star-Spangled Ban-
ner or of defending Old Glory. But, as I have said, I am don-
ning a uniform first and foremost because it is supposed to lift
you a little above the man in the gray flannel suit. It assures
you a place in society which you don't have to earn yourself.
Perhaps this is too cynical a view of myself but, try as I might,
I can't seem to convince myself that I really enjoy giving and
taking orders for any more noble or intelligent reason.

The problem of finding a wife who will accept my career
in the military is probably the most important one which faces
me today. My wife will know, when we marry, that she is to
spend the best years of her life as the wife of an army officer.
She must accept the problems which face an army wife as part
of her life.

I am particularly concerned about my choice of a wife
because she will be my entire life. The only really important
thing in my life after college will be my family. Money and
prestige will be unimportant if I do not have a wife and
family to share them. My one goal in life is to raise a family
properly. If I can provide a good life for my wife and bring
up our children as good Catholics and Americans, I will consider my life a success. I am sure that this sounds corny and a
little phony, but it is true. I suppose the emphasis which I put
on the family is due to a great extent to the influence of my own

parents. Our family has always been a very close one. My mother has built her entire world around the five of us, and Dad is the same way, even though he hates to show it. Because of this, and because of the difficulties I felt with the members of my own age groups, home and the family came to play a part in my life more important than in the lives of most. Even after four years here at Princeton, where everyone believes in hitting all the girls' schools, Bermuda, etc., to have a good time, I still take off for home whenever I get the chance. Of course, I spend most of my time at home out running around, but the main reason I go home is to see the family. Perhaps someday I'll be fortunate enough to see my children come home year after year to see their mother and me. If that happens, I'll feel that my life is a success, even if I'm living in a two-room house.

Aside from her willingness to accept the burdens of my career, the most important thing I look for in a woman is her religion. Since I am a Roman Catholic, I think that it is imperative that my wife be of the same religion. My father was a Protestant until five years ago and, although he was very understanding, I have seen what problems a mixed marriage can create. Now that he is a Catholic, everything goes much more smoothly. If a mixed marriage is necessary, it is almost essential that the wife be the Catholic member. Our religion is an all-pervading influence which is with us every day, all day long. Young children need guidance every day, and if the burden of this guidance falls on the father it is almost impossible for him to do a really adequate job. The mother is the one who is with the children morning, noon, and night. She can teach them their morning and evening prayers. She gets them up on Sunday and dresses them for church. The very nature of the male animal makes it difficult for him to do this, not to mention the fact that he must be away from the house five days a week.

Other than the fact that a Catholic wife would play a vital role in spiritually rearing our children, I also feel that a good

Catholic wife would help *me* greatly in the practice of my religion. Four years here at Princeton have not done my faith any good. Religion in general is seldom mentioned around here, and the Catholic Church in particular takes quite a terrific beating. Of the four boys I have roomed with at one time or another since I came here, not one is a Catholic. One is Jewish, the second is the son of a Presbyterian minister, the third's parents are in the Salvation Army, and the other professes to be an agnostic. Living in this kind of atmosphere is hardly conducive to strengthening one's religion. Mine has taken a terrible beating. I am afraid that if it were to be left in the rather secular atmosphere of the B.O.Q. and the Officer's Club, it would become even weaker. With a good Catholic wife beside me, I hope to be able to rebuild my faith and to pass it on to my children.

I suppose that every man in the world wants to marry a beautiful woman. I would be lying if I said that I didn't. My ideal would be a brown-eyed blonde from a big family. Girls from big families generally know how to cook and how to take care of little children. That sums up what I would consider to be the ideal girl. I don't imagine that I will ever find her, and I doubt that it will worry me too much if I marry a blue-eyed brunette who can't cook a thing. I've always thought that I would marry the woman I fall in love with, no matter who she is or what kind of background she comes from. As I was writing the last sentence it struck me that I nowhere mentioned money as one of my qualifications for the perfect wife. No one in his right mind, of course, would ever turn a woman down just because she is wealthy. However, I have never really thought of marrying into money because, until I came to Princeton, I honestly never knew anybody who was rich. Since freshman year I have met a good many well-to-do Princetonians. Some of them have even become friends of mine. I've also casually met a considerable number of girls who are loaded. But as far as girls from Vassar, Smith, etc., have gone, my policy has been to date them only if absolutely necessary. The only date I've ever had with a rich girl was one with a Vassar freshman last year. It was a blind date, and she turned out to be quite beautiful. But what a pain! All I heard about was her thirty-room house and how *divine* Europe was last summer. I'm sure that she was not representative of the upper-income families of this country. Nevertheless, I'll settle for a wife from a family of moderate means.

By now it should be obvious to the reader that I take my religion very seriously. It is with me day and night, seven days a week. I have had relatively little formal education in my religion. Only my last two years of high school and one year at the University of Santa Clara were spent in Catholic schools. I found that the Christian Brothers who taught in my high school, with their rather liberal approach to religion, were considerably more to my liking than were the stricter Jesuits who teach at the University of Santa Clara. Although I try to be a good Catholic and to follow the precepts of the Church, there are many little things taught by it that I have trouble agreeing with. Despite my doubts, however, I feel that to a great extent I have retained my religion. Princeton has been a terribly corroding influence. But I hope that after I get away from this atmosphere of questioning everything I will be able to regain and strengthen my faith and once more accept what it teaches *in toto*.

One of the chief threats to my peace of mind as a good Catholic has been my relations with the girls I have dated. The most difficult thing for a young Catholic of my age and of my degree of freedom from supervision is his or her relations with the opposite sex. I have been no different than most other college students in this respect. My experience with girls didn't really begin until after I graduated from high school. Not until senior year did I date at all, and then only because, as an officer in the cadet corps, it was expected that I would attend

some of the school's social functions. I had my first real girlfriend that year in the spring, but I was still so bashful that
our relationship remained entirely platonic.

Not until we moved to California, and the fall of my first
semester at Santa Clara College, did I get a driver's license.
This sounds trivial, I'm sure, but, as anyone who thinks about
it will see, it opened a whole new world to me. During the
entire year I spent at college in California I ran and ran, trying
so hard to make up for all the excitement and adventure I'd
missed in high school. I came home every weekend and, never
fail, had at least two dates, one on Friday and one on Saturday.
One crush followed another as I practically drained the local
high school of its available girls. Most of my crushes were on
other army brats. Many of these are still involved in my life in
one way or another, some as married friends, some as just
friends, and some still listed as available. As I look back over
that year, I'm afraid it was a rather pathetic one. I thought
I was such a ladies' man and such a big wheel with my new
college jacket and my big station wagon. I had a lot to learn.
But I suppose the only answer was the one I found: just keep
going, get it out of your system, and learn.

My failure to make the Military Academy and the ago-
nizing decision to start here at Princeton as a freshman once
more were probably the most fortunate things that ever happened to me. My parents realized by then, as I did, that I was
too young to be a sophomore at college. So we decided that
it would be best if I started college all over again and got the
full benefit of the famous Princeton education. Once we'd decided that we could swing it financially, I informed Princeton
that I would enter as a freshman in the class of 1957. That fall
I became for the first time an independent human being.

Among other things, I had never, up to that day, earned an
honest dollar in my life. I had never even had a paper route or
cut lawns for the neighbors. My first decision here at Princeton

was that I had to work and help pay my way through this rich man's school. Freshman year I worked many hours, doing everything from washing windows to parking cars and working behind the desk in the university library. Although I still to this day have never spent an entire summer working, my experience here has helped me to a very great degree to gain some of the self-assurance so necessary in this world.

At Princeton, for the first time in my life, I found myself going to class with boys nearly my own age. For the first time I was beginning to enjoy my classmates and to spend time outside of class with "the boys." I even went out for crew—the first time I ever tried openly to compete with my peers. And for the two and a half years that I continued at it I was even fairly successful. Only the fact that we have the best 150-pound crew in the world kept me from going the whole way to the top.

I had hated school ever since the first day when I'd been sent bawling off to first grade. Now, for a change, I was enjoying it. I still hated to study and have never become much of an intellectual. Even today as a senior I hate to study. But that suddenly wasn't as important as it had been before. I was discovering that there were other things to an education than book and classroom knowledge. After four years here I hold this view even more strongly. Liberal arts majors here really take little away from Princeton except the fabled well-rounded personality of which Princeton is so proud. I personally have my doubts about the advantages of a Princeton education. This university admits over seven hundred of the top college students of the country every year. And while they are here, the majority of them never get an opportunity to absorb any useful knowledge whatever. I will admit that Old Nassau turns out fine graduates, but think how much better they would be if they had taken at least one course somewhere along in their education that would be useful to them in later life. The argument that Princeton has turned out top men with its present system is so much bunk. The university's prestige and long history simply attract the most capable students in the country. It would be hard for Princeton not to have successful graduates.

Right now I am not quite sure whether I would send my sons here to school or not. There seems little doubt that an even moderately intelligent Princeton graduate has many advantages in business, government, or the professions that graduates from most other colleges do not have. I somehow feel that when a prospective employer sees that one applicant is from Princeton and the other from State College, he will almost certainly choose the one from P. U. Still, I can't quite convince myself that prestige and money are the most important things in our lives. Wouldn't it be better for my children to go to a Catholic university and build strong foundations for their faith? I have learned from the mistakes my parents have made. Perhaps I can save my children the doubt, fear, and uncertainty that gnaw at a young man's soul when he is thrown to the Princeton Tiger. But this is a decision I'll have to make when I can look back and see what lasting effects Princeton has had on me.

One thing that my Princeton experience *has* contributed to my development, especially through the sports I have participated in, has been a very great increase in my self-confidence. It has helped me immeasurably to know that, in some respects at least, I'm as good as anyone. The only trouble with that realization is that I now find myself on the edge of a new life in which I will have to prove myself all over again. Never really having held a job outside of the university for any length of time, I still have doubts about my ability to do so. I am out to become one of the best officers in the United States Army. My purpose is not to impress anyone else; all I want to do is to show myself that I can do as well as or better than the next man. I am my own sharpest critic.

To come back to the problem of my relations with the other sex. My experience at necking and petting four years ago was nil. Now it is fairly extensive. It is a rare date at Princeton when one doesn't do a little necking at least. We go to great pains to pick girls who look like hot stuff, and nothing is more amusing than the fellow who has a very sexy-looking date who turns a cold shoulder to his advances. In a case like that the whole weekend is ruined, even if we do beat Yale. Ninety-five per cent of the guys here—at least for their weekend dates—are just looking for that "cheap physical stuff." And I am no exception. I am cooped up here like everyone else and when the rare date does come along it's only natural to look for a little display of affection. Besides relieving some of the unavoidable biological tensions, it's good for the ego that a girl is willing to pet with you.

As far as more serious affairs are concerned, for the first two years here at Princeton I was really unblemished. Since then, I'm afraid, I've become a real roué, a man of the world for sure. I am no longer innocent in any sense of the word, and I'm very sorry for it. Pre-marital relations are strictly against my religion and for my few lapses I have paid plenty in sorrow and worry. I hope and pray that it will never happen again until my marriage. God willing, my own weak will will become stronger.

As far as the woman situation at present is concerned, it doesn't look good. I have been dating a woman much older than myself who is now talking of marriage. My relations with her have been an entirely new experience for me. She works in town and at first I spent three or four evenings a week at her house. Since she is a really wonderful person, it has been hard to shut her out of my life completely. As much as we have enjoyed each other's company, I'm afraid I sensed from the beginning that as far as marriage would go we were not meant for each other. Now that I have been able to conquer the fascination which she held for me at first, the experience has become just one more of the incidents that have gone into making me a man. Some of these incidents I am not proud of and would hope in the future to avoid. But, in a way, I'm glad they happened.

I don't know what kind of a picture all these rambling thoughts and confessions have given the reader. Whatever it is, let me add to it a few words about my rather extroverted personality. In high school I was quiet, withdrawn, and meek. Now I am by far the noisiest person in my university eating club. Fortunately I have a very quick wit, which smooths most people down so that my noise doesn't irritate them too much. I always try, unconsciously, to dominate the conversation— even when the table is large enough for twelve people. My tongue has been sharpened over the last years to the point where I can match any of my classmates with fast and funny retorts. Actually, I probably get away with riding people so much because most of them don't take me seriously. Still, I have made a lot of enemies, and I will leave here with no really close friends. As a matter of fact, I don't think I have ever had a bosom buddy. I always have many acquaintances and friends, but no one whom I am likely to feel close to in the years after we have left here. I don't quite know what the reason is for this inability of mine to make and keep close friends. It is probably my big mouth and my tendency to criticize everyone unduly. Now that my college days are over and I realize many of my shortcomings, I hope that I can change my ways and learn to live and work with people better than I have in the past.

I haven't proved very much by all this chitchat, but perhaps you who are reading this book will know a little better what makes at least one member of my generation—me—tick. I am not typical of the boys I know, but then, who *is* typical? In the next thirty years you may read about my promotion up through the grades; who knows, I may even be President, although my religion really precludes that. You may also read about my dishonorable discharge for cowardice or nonperformance of duty. I really don't know what's going to happen to me or the country. All I know is that if I have to die in a war, it will probably be the war which marks the end of our way of life. If we have peace, the future doesn't look too dark to me. There is much which can and will be done to carry out the values that America stands for, both here at home and throughout the world. In spite of my rather negative attitudes, I really have great faith in my classmates and all their peers all over the nation. I am convinced that they have what it takes. As for myself, I'm afraid I still don't know. Only time and a lot of work and prayers will answer that.

TO BECOME A MAN

I HAVE SPENT THE LAST FOUR YEARS of my life attempting to remedy the results of my first nineteen years. Yet I do not in any way consider myself a rebel. For my particular sense of perspective this would be much too dramatic. In the years since I entered college I have simply had to wake up to reality and to develop my own way of looking at the world around me. Up to that time my thinking and actions had been decided for me. At Princeton I have learned to grow up. This experience of awakening self-awareness, combined with the built-in reactions of my first nineteen years, has given me the personality I now have, and the opinions I now possess.

I was born in 1934 in a small Texas town, in what is known as a nice middle-class neighborhood. By 1953 I had lived in ten different towns and cities, from New York to Rio de Janeiro. Along with the ten different places of residence went eleven different schools. Each new school was always the same: being led into an overheated classroom and looking at waves of new faces. I suppose most of the faces were just looking at me with curiosity. To me they all seemed hostile and animal-like. In the first and second grades, in the United States, I was the class bully. In South America I was the local punching bag. The plane trip south of the border was so rough that I was sick most of the way. When I wasn't sick, I read. *Bomba the Jungle Boy in the Swamp of Death* was my first independent adventure with the printed word. I remember the trip as one long scared feeling.

At the airport we were met by my father's business associates. "How do you like it here?" they asked, grinning down at my younger brother and me. How could I tell whether or not I liked it? I'd only just arrived. There was a long cyclone fence and everybody wore gabardine topcoats. The next thing was a bitterly cold building with long white tile corridors. We were fingerprinted. A strange foreign man pressed my hand roughly on a pad. My father took me to wash up. The water was so cold it hurt. Our next stop was another hotel. Somebody found a house for us. It seemed to me that it took us a week to locate it.

School was really odd. Morning classes in Spanish and afternoon classes in English. Because I didn't know any Spanish, I was put back a grade. The next three years at that school were a succession of skinned knees, short pants, and hiding behind bushes from the other kids. I learned to play soccer. A girl named Virginia told me about number one and number two. She lent me *Huckleberry Finn,* which I never returned. I drew constantly. Always war pictures, with tanks and airplanes, Japs, Germans, and Russians, good guys and bad guys.

One day I took my toy sailboat to the park. It had a United States flag on it. A man there told me that I shouldn't have a flag like that on my boat. I stared at him and felt like pushing him into the pond. Then there was a revolution. My parents came to get my brother and me at school. I'd just won a game of marbles. As we drove through the city, we were caught in a military convoy. Between two armored cars we drove past the naval academy. There were big holes in the walls and the shutters hung askew. The iron rail fence was flattened where the tanks had gone through. All that afternoon we stayed home. The sirens kept screaming as ambulances went by. Dad went to work to help guard the plant.

My brother slept. I hid between our twin beds, with my bow, my arrows and a slingshot beside me. I was scared stiff. The first man who came over the garden wall was going to get shot! The next day our maid's brother came by and told us how, with his knife, he'd torn up a streetcar's seats and had helped to turn it over and set it on fire. I couldn't understand why.

With some neighborhood boys I built a puppet theater. We gave a show, but I never got my share of the money. The other boys said they'd had to pay some expenses, but I knew that they just didn't want to give me any. But why? Wasn't that dishonest? Didn't they go to the same church as I did?

I started to prepare for my first Confession and Communion. I was scared again. What would it be like? It meant so much. Could I actually have God in me? Religion frightened me.

We went back home to the States and lived in Texas. I went to school and was promoted from the fifth to the sixth grade. I began refusing to wear my glasses for fear the other kids would laugh at me. They did anyway. I couldn't play baseball because I couldn't even see the pitcher's mound. I fanned out every time. Even the girls laughed. Dad was always away on business. The war wasn't yet over and we still had rationing. That was strange after Latin America.

"Always be a little gentleman," I'd been told. Once I lost my temper with a boy and called him a Nazi. He didn't understand my apology. I was in tears when I made it. He never apologized to me after calling me a dirty name. We were always fighting in that neighborhood. Once I wanted to set off firecrackers with the other kids. Mom said it was too dangerous and wouldn't let me. She lit them for me.

There was a boy, Joel, who lived three doors down the street and whom I cordially detested. My friend Everett and I were chasing him one day, but he outran us and ducked into his front door. Everett said that was O.K. since Jews could always run faster than Gentiles. I learned about prejudice.

My family kept on moving. We went back to the town in Illinois where we had lived before the South American jaunt. I recognized all my old acquaintances. They told me how I'd changed: I used to hit everybody, and now it was the other way around. Now, at last, I finally found out what football and basketball were. In junior high school it really shocked me to see the short trunks the boys played in. An athletic support was an object of vulgarity and horror. The kids used to tell jokes which I laughed at but didn't understand. I became an altar boy and lived in holy terror of dropping the big book which I carried. My brother did drop it once and it made quite a noise.

We moved again, this time up to New York. I went to a private school where I was dropped back a grade because I hadn't had Latin. But I liked it anyway. I finally made the baseball team. I learned to broad jump and shot-put and got a medal in each. And my range of friends began to widen. I used to walk through vacant lots and see things on the ground which looked like white balloons. Then doubts were dispelled by my mother's present of a little book entitled *In Training*. The cover depicted a group of healthy boys playing football. Great idea, I thought, now I can learn to make a drop kick. The book, however, was quite different from what I'd expected and, instead, I learned about sex.

Again we moved. This time it was out in the country, near a small village. For the first time in my thirteen years I went to a parochial school. The old routine of fighting the school bully never materialized. Everybody liked me and I liked them. For the first time in my life I began to study and found that I enjoyed it. The religious aspect both appealed to me and bothered me. Yet I accepted it unquestioningly. Those nuns were indeed wonderful people.

Then I entered an all-boys Catholic high school. I loathed it from the start. There were about eleven hundred assorted thugs, animals, and introverts at that place, from all over the New York area. The priests and brothers ruled with a heavy hand. Looking back on it now I realize that the strictness was necessary in order to keep that mob of little gangsters from taking the place apart brick by brick. Still, it was quite a shock to see priests, for whom as a group I had always had the greatest respect, actually striking us. I think in some instances it was deserved, but to see an idealized man of God *hit* a friend of mine in the face four times for cheating on an exam was quite a shock. We had religion classes every day. I took everything that was said quite literally. Hell was a horrible place where you could go for almost any infraction. I realize now that I was probably the only one there who took it all so literally. The priests were using a scatter-gun technique in dispensing religious precepts. They overloaded both barrels and then let fly, in the hope that at least some of it would stick to their unruly pupils. In spite of my absorption of all this religious teaching, I began to dislike it. We were hustled into chapel constantly. Each year, on the occasion of the big religious retreat before Easter Week, a sin-killing preacher would treat us all to a spectacle of religious oratory. I became overscrupulous in spite of my genuine abhorrence of this ranting performance. Still, I prayed constantly. I think I was scared not to.

My mother still dominated my home life, since Dad, as usual, had little time for us. This wasn't his fault. He was working hard, because he wanted to make us happy and comfortable. Unfortunately he failed to strike a balance between home and the office. He tried to teach me to drive a car but then gave up. I was sixteen at the time and wanted to get my junior license. Mother put off teaching me. I had always been told that I was not of a mechanical turn of mind. My brother could take clocks apart and put them together (more or less).

I had trouble turning doorknobs. When I was finally taught to drive, I received healthy admonishments at every turn. My mistakes were recited to family friends amidst bursts of laughter. I finally took my test and passed. I was nearly eighteen. Every time I got behind the wheel I used to say a little prayer. I had no self-confidence. Religion was becoming a crutch.

About drinking. I believed that if it was not wrong, it was at least "an occasion of sin." One drink would render me incapable of self-control. Getting drunk was a sin. Our religion textbooks moralized about the dangers of it. My parents drank at home. Under their watchful eyes I occasionally had a weak one. The slightest mistake in my grammar while drinking my watery Scotch and soda brought (or so I thought) raised eyebrows. My schoolmates drove at night, had dates, and drank. I believed that to combine these three diversions was wrong. I had dates, yes, but not at night (at least not until the latter part of my senior year). At parties I refused to drink. I was a square. I had few real friends. But then, as I now realize, most of the people at the school were pretty undesirable anyway. Still, I felt left out. The friends I did have were, I believe, pretty fine boys. Yet there was a gulf between us. They drove at night and drank at parties. I freely admit that I can never condone drunken driving, but in those days I was overly scrupulous socially, as well as religiously.

"Are you a virgin?" a young lady asked me my senior year. I nearly drove off the road at that. "Is your mother coming to give you a ride home from school today?" an animal classmate jeered at me. The Senior Prom was ghastly. My first date at night in the car. I was horribly nervous. All through the dance I worried about driving home. Suppose I got a flat tire? Could I fix it? To my date I didn't pay much attention. Other couples went bar-hopping after the dance. We drove straight home.

I began to question myself and all that I knew or had experienced. What was wrong with me? I had been encounter-

ing a new type of life. I had begun to go to dances at the
country club. All the people there of my age went to prep
schools. My only prep school was Arthur Murray's. They
dressed so well. They smoked and drank. They were polite and
well-bred. They were also as phony and as shallow as they
could possibly be. But I didn't see this. All I saw was the outside veneer. I was a "perfect gentleman" and as such was
ridiculous. I realize now that they were not as sure of themselves as I thought they were. They had just learned to cover
it up. I couldn't do this. It was a new world, divorced from
my Catholic, high-school existence. I liked it very much. Still,
I wasn't a part of that world either. Andover, Exeter, Farming-
ton were just names. I had never been to Europe. What did
the sixth form mean? Was it like the sixth grade? To tell the
truth, I still don't know. But at that time it meant very much
to know or at least to pretend that I knew. The conflict between
these two worlds hit me squarely. Which one held a place for
me? Neither. By pretending to belong to the prep-school,
country-club world, I was not being me. And I rejected the
thought of the high-school world.

I continued to be preoccupied with religion. I saw sin
in everything I did. My home upbringing and my travelling
about so much had brought and kept me very close to my
parents. I obeyed them unquestioningly. Any desire of an
older person was my command. I carried this habit of obedience over into my religion. It was a preoccupation with form
combined with a genuine, intense religious conviction. At my
high school the form was given too much precedence. As I
began occasionally to rebel against my parents, I also started
to rebel against religious form, at least mentally. My constant
dependence on my parents and my religion was sapping my
will power. I saw this and was frightened. Yet I couldn't break
away. Then I realized something. I was about to graduate.

I wanted to go to Princeton. I had always wanted to go
there ever since I had first seen it while I was in the eighth

grade. I wanted it. The ivy, the spirit, the old buildings. I wanted it all. The priests in school couldn't understand. I was asked, "Why do you want to go to Princeton?" I had no answer. I just did. Must there *be* a reason? "Does it have better educational opportunities than Holy Cross or Notre Dame?" It did, I knew it did. I said "yes" to my questioner. "You'll lose your Faith," I was told. I felt like telling them that if I went another year to a Catholic school, I would lose it anyway. What difference did it make? I said nothing. It was my first mental rejection of the past four years.

My parents supported my views. The Dean at school showed some reluctance at writing a recommendation. Dad straightened him out. I was accepted at Princeton. It was the happiest day of my life. Princeton also came to represent to me a chance to break with home. A new start. Maybe I'd find a place to belong. Maybe I'd grow up. I still believed in miracles.

At high-school graduation I won medals by the handful— even the religion medal. I saw the people I had graduated with. Very few friends. Out there was the person who had scrawled "He's an elf" on the election poster which I had put up while making an unsuccessful bid for School President. A football Neanderthal had won. In that mass of tasseled mortarboards, also, was the individual who had expressed an intense longing to knock my teeth out. They could all go to Hell. I was getting out of their world. I never wanted to return. I couldn't run out of the auditorium fast enough.

I arrived at Princeton as possibly the most ignorant and callow person who had trodden that soil since George Washington had chased out the Redcoats. My first night I got drunk. On only a quart of beer. A bunch of us sang songs and vied with one another in telling the worst dirty jokes. I felt good. I was starting to belong.

Football weekends were fun. Parties galore. I was a college man, so I thought. I screamed myself hoarse for the Orange and the Black. I found a girl in town I could kiss. It wasn't the first time I had kissed an agreeable female. I just didn't think it was a sin now. In high school I had believed it to be horribly dangerous to my immortal soul. I came to kick myself for all the lost opportunities. I was trying to belong. Desperately trying. I thought I was succeeding. Girls were fun. But football games, drinking, and singing dirty songs were greater. After the strict discipline of my four high-school years, college seemed like a holiday. I worked during the week and got drunk on weekends. I still made excellent marks. The girl in town started going out with a sophomore. I started to get my old self-doubts again.

I still went to church every Sunday and prayed frequently. My religion still was a crutch. Yet it now assumed a different aspect. I became more tolerant of other people. So tolerant that I felt myself becoming a jellyfish. Protestants and Jews were people just like me. They had always been just like me, but I had never fully realized it.

Sophomore year I joined an eating club. I found out a lot about myself that I had been blind to since arriving at Princeton. I was not a Joe College. I still lacked the polish of my contemporaries. I was influenced by others whom I considered my friends. The solid group we had had as freshmen began to fragment as we moved to different clubs and dormitories. The exclusive clubs wouldn't look at me. I was not tweedy, I realized. I was not smooth. This was apparent, too, in my relations with girls. I was an overly sincere, overly nice kid. I joined a club of no particular distinction. Not bad, not good. I went in because of friends in it. It was a mistake. In the years to come I would grow to dislike these "friends." Something was wrong with me. I tried to be tolerant of everyone and everybody. By doing so I lost grasp of the essence of good taste.

My parents still held much control over me. I respected and loved them. In their eyes I was still a kid. I knew they were right. Yet I felt differently towards them. I wanted to be independent. At home I felt invisible walls around me. That first summer vacation was torture. They didn't make me happy, and I know I made them unhappy. I still went to dances at the country club. It was good to be able to tell people that I was going to Princeton. But I still wasn't a part of that life. I realized it more than ever. My peculiar background set me apart from any and every group I had ever met. Even at Princeton.

Junior year I proceeded to get absolutely soused every weekend in an attempt, crazy though it was, to belong. I would pass out at parties and try to be a "fast" guy with the women. The high point of that fall was when I painted "Hate Yale" on my bare chest and tried to shock everyone I could find. I wanted to be a party boy, a good-time Charlie. I was quite proud of my feat. Late in the fall I was elected a junior officer at my club. I helped to arrange the annual Christmas party and then, my duties done, got drunk and passed out. I soon realized my mistake. I lost the election for Club President by a narrow margin. The reason was that many members considered me irresponsible because of my drinking. I woke up fast. I had come a long way since high school. From one extreme to another. From boy pure-heart to boy drunk. Again I was in a mess. Every attempt I had made to conform, to belong, had failed. I belonged to no group. For the first time in three years I started to think rationally. What could I do with myself? It was time to face facts and to become a man. By trying to belong I was merely denying my own personality. I spent weeks in thinking.

That summer I went to South America to study. There I was really on my own. I could find out what I really was. I didn't pretend to be something I was not. I was myself and I found that the people I met liked it. Aside from a fruitless amorous entanglement, in which I nearly lost my head, I learned quite a bit. I began to be happy with myself. I was interested in my work and threw myself into it. I was proud of myself and what I was doing. I looked at the world around me with open eyes and liked what I saw. I liked life. My early sojourn in Latin America bore fruit. I found that I understood the people. I liked them very much. I was independent of home. I was me. I resolved that it would remain that way. I drank much less. I became the center of my universe. Belonging no longer mattered. I thought over my past mistakes and resolved never to let myself fall again into such a quagmire. I saw religion with a different viewpoint. What truly mattered was the inner feeling. Religion was an intensely personal thing, and nobody had any right to tell me what to believe.

Upon returning home I found that my transition to the Anglo-Saxon world was quite simple. I could hold my belief in myself in the United States as well as in South America. My environment need not be a crutch or a hobble. Religion either. Take out of life what you can, I made up my mind, but put something in for what you subtract. My parents noticed my new self-reliance. A change of scene, new thoughts, even buying airplane tickets had helped me to develop. A supreme mental effort had also helped.

My senior year was one of adjusting my new-found personality to my environment. It was a year filled with many problems and decisions, as well as with much hard work. I wrote my thesis with enthusiasm and eagerness. What I had learned in South America, from my research as well as through my new perspective on life, enabled me to do a thorough, mature job. I came to like scholarship not only as an end in itself, but also as a means of broadening my world view. I became aware of my ignorance and read more voraciously than ever. My contacts with people increased as I became a responsible club officer. I learned to compromise with life and my fellow man. I was no longer motivated by fear or self-doubt in my search for knowledge and companionship. Compromise, I discovered, was not a sign of weakness. Rather, it was an indication of strength. It is easy to be a rebel, either actively through iconoclasm or passively by total withdrawal. Life is what you make it, but in any case you have to live with it. To live each moment to the full in an intelligent, rational manner became my goal.

I suffered disappointments, to be sure. The realization that the members of my club did not have the same ideas as I did about improving the membership was a severe blow. The club which I had idealistically hoped to improve seemed to have let me down. Then I recognized the fact that the club —the majority of its membership and I—had never been in tune at all. I had failed to see this because of my inability to look at a situation with both eyes open. I had seen something in the club that had never been there. I had only my own blindness to blame. I grew up a little more. Then I was no longer hurt. I had no right to expect other people to hold the same dreams that I did, just as I had no right to wish to "belong" to their dreams. It didn't bother me. I was myself.

I fell in love, really in love, for the first time in my life. The sharing of such an experience opened my eyes a bit more. That another person, a living, thinking, feeling person, could be one in spirit with me was a never-ending source of amazement. For the first time in my life I touched another human soul. I learned about compromise, give and take, the beauty of the glint of even teeth in a loving smile. A kiss, a caress, an eternal embrace.

Religion remained a great force in my life, yet it wasn't orthodox Catholic belief. The religious sense in me was too deep and entangled for that. I did things not at all condoned by the Church. Yet I couldn't see a merciful, almighty, all-knowing God sending me to Hell. Religion was no longer a fear or a crutch. It was an all-pervading consciousness of the Almighty and a sense of unending process.

The struggle to break away from my family continued, but my mother and father were steadily losing ground. They came to realize that I was no longer a child. But it was not easy. I was torn between my duty to them and my duty to myself. The latter obligation won. My mother and I had always been quite close, but now she saw that closeness fading. My father began to think of those lost years when he was not able to cement that comradeship which should exist between a boy and a man. They tried to hold on to me, but, I think, decided that if they tried any harder they would lose me. The conflict was heightened by my new love. I believe that they had never liked any girl whom I had dated. Maybe this was jealousy. It was most certainly because they wanted the best for me. They just had to find out that I had very definite ideas of my own as to what was best for me. The domestic battles were severe. I found myself hating them. Yet I had to admit that I had been remiss on many accounts, especially in the amount of money I was spending. But suddenly I was free. Another crutch was gone. And gone with it was hate.

Soon I will be graduated and hurled into what is graphically described as the "cold world." I realize that no one will do me any favors, but somehow I'm not worried. Admittedly it will be unlike the incubator existence of my first twenty-three years. But at long last I'm ready for it, even though I'm a bit late. I firmly believe that I can take life. The purpose of my being on earth is to develop whatever qualities and abilities I have in order to become fully alive, to become a man in every sense of the word. Most people, I am convinced, never learn this. If we are given talents, we are expected to develop them. If we are given life, we are meant to live it. This is not hedonism. Living implies certain obligations to the one who is alive.

One of these is duty to one's fellow man. Your happiness is as nothing if in attaining it you take happiness from someone else. This poses a difficult problem if you think about it. No action is ever completely good or completely bad. Out of war can come valor and heroism. So can selfishness and cowardice. All we can do is to act in that way which seems the best at the time, then hope that we have done correctly. Be prepared to take the bad if it comes. Be equally prepared to enjoy the good. Overpreoccupation with either leads to ulcers. My high-school preoccupation with the religious ideal led to thoughts of suicide.

What I want out of life is simply to live it, nothing more, in a way so as to develop my every sense and perception. My fellow man comes into the picture also. By living life one does set an example. I am not being naïve. I realize what people are and can be. I have seen them at their best and also at their worst, be they holy people, drunks, idealists, cynics, or prostitutes. I would like to go into university teaching or the State Department. In either of these fields a person can find self-expression, cherishment of an ideal, and communication with others.

I believe that I am a patriot. Nothing annoys me more than the svelte young thing at a cocktail party who passes her time sipping a Martini (which she probably thinks is risqué) and discussing the crassness of materialistic America in comparison with sophisticated Paris. Princeton harbors the male of this species. He hides behind horn-rimmed glasses and an inferiority complex while tearing at pragmatic, utilitarian Uncle Sam and extolling the virtues of free, untrammeled Europe, last refuge of the spiritual. Equally deplorable is the professional tourist who believes that only in Europe can be found scenic beauty and good wine. Chances are that he has never been further west than the Bronx. Our nation is quite young and, considering its youth, has done a great deal to alter the map of history. True, we do not have the culture of Europe, but

* See: Maritain: Reflections on America
Scribner's - 1958.

then, that continent did have a bit of a head start on us. We have our poets, painters, and authors. Admittedly, Racine and Corneille have a great reputation, but they have had the benefit of centuries to enhance the beauty of their works. Time has a peculiar way of putting a rosy gloss on men and things. America's sin, if you can call it that, is in being young. The future is still to come. I am proud of my country and want to serve it in any way I can. Of course, spending time in the army is no picnic. But then, if life were a picnic it might not be so interesting.

Our system of education is unfortunately set up in such a way as to idealize the foreign. Of course, the Pledge of Allegiance to the flag is still observed in most schools. But something is lacking and manifests itself at the college level in a type of cynicism concerning patriotism. Patriotism can never be bad taste. Yet many people seem to think that it is "corny." This is something which we, as a nation, should realize and correct.

United States universities, while they offer magnificent opportunities for learning, seem to me to fall short in respect to their faculties. There are more scholars than teachers. I mean by this that there are few people here who really *teach*. The devoted few who do are teachers because they succeed in communicating their love of a subject to their students, engendering in them a genuine love of learning. This communication is the essence of teaching. Most professors think of themselves firstly as scholars. They accept a position at a university in order to have a chance to study or to provide for their families. This is not bad conduct, but *is* bad teaching practice. They fail to grasp the essence of teaching and by so doing fail to arouse the minds of their pupils as effectively as they should.

The purpose of an education, especially in the liberal arts, is to make a person think about himself, the universe, and time. It is to make him want to realize his capabilities. Unfortunately this does not appear to be recognized by most people. "What do you learn to do?" people ask of college students. The reason this question is asked is that we are a young nation, constantly building and rebuilding ourselves. Therefore, something without a utilitarian purpose seems to many a waste of time. This will change as we become more mature as a people. An educated man is a patient man. A pseudo-intellectual who rejects America because of her youth is not only impatient and uneducated but also a bore.

It is a tendency of youth to want simple solutions. Many people never cease to want to see things in blacks and whites. This is an especially strong tendency among the pseudo-intellectuals mentioned above. They obscure the real facts by their insistent pursuit of some ideal, of something that should be. For example, speakers are invited to lecture on college campuses without regard for what their appearance may do to the university's reputation. "Freedom of speech" is pursued with such vigor that the obligations implied in the very grant of that freedom take a back seat. Many people are so anxious to be tolerant that in their efforts to show their "liberality" towards those of another race or creed, they themselves become prejudiced. Others try so hard to avoid conformity by being "different" that they become stereotyped Bohemians. In so doing they not only lose their own individuality but become the greatest conformists of all. In my four years at Princeton I have met only one person whom I consider to be a true intellectual. The others whom I have met or heard of are, in my opinion, escapists and phonies. To live is to strike a compromise with life.

I consider it dangerous to judge my own generation in terms of my experiences at Princeton. This institution represents but a minute segment of America. The East is but a part of a greater whole. However, in view of my travelling, my reading, and my conversations with people of various backgrounds, I believe that a few generalizations can be made. On the surface we appear to be rather complacent and self-satisfied. I wonder if this complacency is nothing but a protective shield to hide our basic insecurity. Threats of war, the draft, loss of identity in a big corporation, loss of a spiritual ideal, and the pressures of an ever-evolving mechanical civilization all make the individual feel isolated and overawed in daily life. Sometimes complacency is shattered in subtle as well as in overt ways. Panty raids, juvenile delinquency, drunkenness, intellectual escapism are manifestations of this. We appear to rush through life so that we need never look at ourselves and question what we are doing.

God, I think, must be a pretty nice guy. This statement is not intended to be comical or facetious. It is simply my conception of the Creator. He allowed man to develop and to decay with a countless number of civilizations: the Sumerians, the Hittites, the Babylonians, the Persians, the Greeks, the Romans, the Mayas, the Aztecs. He gave to man life. Man tried to do what the Source of Life desired. Man saw Him as a tree trunk, a dragon, or a man on a cross. God was cajoled, propitiated, adored, villified. Civilizations crumbled and new ones took their place. God was still God. In spite of man and whatever he did, God continued to shower blessings on the being he had created. The earth kept turning, the sun remained shining.

THE INDIVIDUAL AT BAY

Society today is being pervaded by an insidious and consuming quality: regimentation. It is against this dominant fact of the twentieth century that my life until now has been a struggle. I realize that the price of society is some kind of compulsion. As far as I am concerned, however, the only valid and creative compulsion is that which is self-imposed; any other is exterior to the individual and destructive of his sense of personal responsibility.

My earliest recollection is of a scene in my parents' home, when I was four or five. We were living in a large apartment in a high-rent district of a large city. The apartment had a long hall, off the middle of which was a white tile bathroom. I remember running up and down that hall, passing the massive white-clothed form of my Irish nurse, bent over scrubbing the bathroom floor. Each time I scurried by I would gleefully pound that vast posterior of hers, and then race down to the other end of the hall. She, in turn, would grimace and feign anger, which made the maneuver all the more fun. I remember her fondly, especially since in those early years I had little contact with my mother, and none with my father.

Mother never seemed to have much time for my brother and me, and father was an imposing figure with a vest and a gold watch chain. One Christmas Eve, while seated on his lap, I broke it—and thereby spoiled the holiday. Once, shortly after my family had bought and moved into an imposing graystone house in that same fashionable district, my brother and I somehow contracted scarlet fever. To make it more convenient for the ugly, unpleasant special nurse who had been engaged to look after us, the doctor suggested that during our period of quarantine we occupy my parents' sleeping quarters. We did, but I don't think my father ever forgave us for putting him out of his bedroom. During this illness I also recall one evening when both parents peeked into the room to say good night before leaving for a party. Father was dressed like a penguin, in a peculiar black suit. Mother was gowned in flowing turquoise and seemed more beautiful and untouchable than ever. I remember imploring her to stay, to sit at the other end of the room; she wouldn't get sick, I said. All I wanted was to look at her. But no, they left for the ball.

Soon after, my father enrolled me in a private day school for boys. It was supposed that I would be properly educated there, and consort with the "right kind" of boys. I did.

In the years between fourth and seventh grade my home life became almost intolerable. My performance at school was mediocre, but that did not concern my parents. I still recall with horror those nights at the Family Dinner Table. During this period the last of our nurses had left, and the two boys were being educated in manners at Table. My father was unbelievable: he would preside like a High Inquisitor; he was loud, unpleasant, hypercritical, irrepressible, and dogmatic. His favorite preoccupation was the castigation of womankind in general, and mother in particular. Occasionally mother would leave the table in tears, but more often he would shift his unpredictable, yet consistent, anger to my brother and myself. Sometimes his ranting made me ill, and I tried to invent stories for myself to distract my attention from him so that I would not vomit on my plate. But he always seemed to know when my mind wandered from his diatribe, and would snap me back sharply.

One of his favorite subjects was the high cost of sending two boys to an expensive private school. The fact was that he was a moderately wealthy merchant and that his business was doing quite well. Yet he insisted that we boys bring our lunch from home, buy secondhand books, and, what hurt most, that we not be permitted to take milk and crackers with the rest of the boys at the midmorning recess. Almost every evening he repeated his bitter, irrational, and often cutting remarks. At one point his raving was so vicious that our maid quit, protesting that she could not work in a home whose master was so unpleasant to his family. My mother, however, accepted it all. She is a very permissive person. Her distinguishing characteristic, indeed, is that she can accept anything—providing she has had three Martinis before dinner.

During those years I was placed on an allowance of twenty-five cents a week, about one quarter of what my classmates were receiving. Finally, seeing no other way to supplement my income, I began to steal. But it was not simply stealing money to buy things. I remember leaving the table one evening seething with distaste for the autocrat at the dinner table. My father never struck me, but destroyed me nightly. I wanted to get back at him. He was always talking about money, so— I wanted to get him where it would hurt. I took change from the pile on the mantel in my parents' room, half hoping that I would be caught and could tell him why I stole his money. But he never caught me. I expanded my thefts to dollar bills from his wallet. As I reflect now, I *must* have been trying to be discovered, to be able to blurt out my antagonism, to take my punishment, and to make him modify his attitude at home. I took more money than I needed. The war was on in earnest at that time, and there were fervent appeals for investment in war bonds. I stole so much money that I couldn't spend it all, and bought at least three small-denomination bonds.

And finally I *was* caught—but by my mother. While cleaning my room, she discovered the securities and sought an explanation. I admitted everything. However, fearing that it would merely provide further ammunition for my father's dinner-table diatribes, she kept the matter from him. She made me swear never to steal again, and I did. But I was accustomed to having a great deal of pocket money and soon began stealing again, this time from the pockets of boys at school, when they had hung up their clothes during athletics. Eventually I was apprehended at this, too. My thefts were never made public, and though my mother was informed, my father, again, was not. Instead, I was sent to the school psychologist for protracted sessions lasting about a year. He was a pleasant man who listened very sympathetically.

My contacts with the school psychologist resulted in two new understandings which, in modified form, I still retain. Of course, his first objective was to stop my kleptomania. I was about thirteen years old at the time and approaching a certain degree of rationality. I couldn't accept his first suggestion, which was that I should not steal because it was wrong. "Wrong," in itself, meant very little to me at the time. After that he spoke in terms which did make sense to me. He said that one ought not to steal because, sooner or later, one is bound to be caught. Being caught, and the inevitable publicity involved, would "outlaw" me from my friends and would render whatever goals I might have difficult if not impossible. Don't steal, because if you do, you will lose whatever you want. And on this basis I gave up stealing. In later years I have buttressed this rather weak ethic with other sanctions and, in fact, have never stolen again.

In his study of me, the psychologist administered many tests. He told me something which I had never even suspected: that I was a rather gifted child! Until that time, my grades had been undistinguished, and I had languished through my studies. He told me that I should be leading my class. Within two months I was in the first position, which I maintained for the rest of my school career. And even at college I have been able to stay in the top ten per cent of my class. I owe much to that Pickwickesque little man.

After I had given up stealing it was sports that became the outlet for my pent-up feelings of aggression. Being large and strong for my age, I found football especially appealing. And I did well at it. Practice I found slightly annoying. I always wanted to attack. In practice I could never let go, for fear of hurting my friends. But in the Saturday-morning games my blood literally seethed. Unshaven and silent for days before a game, I really gloried in ripping through the opposition and nailing the ball carrier to the ground. In my junior year I received quite some recognition from the city press, and was elected varsity captain for the following year. I had been after that job for four years, not only on the playing fields, but in the corridors and classrooms. With it came next to the highest prestige in the school. The biggest job, that of president of the student government, was almost mine, too; but I dropped out of the running at the last minute because it looked as though the election would degenerate into a popularity poll; and on that basis, I feared, I would emerge second best.

In the spring of my third year of prep school, at the age of sixteen, I had my first love affair. I met a girl whose beauty, passion, wit and sensitivity completely engulfed me. Our first encounter was at one of those innumerable Christmas dances that the subdeb set attended. For sixteen, she had a rather full figure and a perfectly groomed bell of jet hair, framing exquisitely small features punctuated by tiny, deep, incisive eyes. We met at subsequent parties and fell deeply in love.

I believe it is possible to become more completely infatuated with another person during the throes of adolescence than at any other time of life. During that period one has a range of interests which, compared with those of an older person, more travelled and educated, is much more restricted.

At that time of life it is still possible to find another person who has the same interests and who views different facets of life in the same manner. Later, with an expanded horizon, it becomes impossible for any two people to find in each other so perfect a complement of themselves. It seemed that between this girl and me there was not a subject which we had not independently considered and resolved in the same manner. And we were perfectly adjusted sexually, though in retrospect, I believe she was somewhat more experienced than I.

The only impediment in our relationship was distance. She lived thirty miles away in one of the city's pretentious suburbs. I had no car, and my father would not permit me the use of his. We solved this problem, though, by visiting each other on alternate weekends. One weekend she would come into town and stay with friends; the next weekend I would stay at her home as a house guest. Between these times we would write letters, sometimes two a day, as well as compose some very bad poetry. She tended toward free verse with monumental Freudian symbolism, while mine sounded, I suppose, like Edgar Guest with a stomach-ache.

As the weeks passed, we became more and more infatuated with each other. Our physical relationship reached an impasse: we had progressed through the usual necking into very serious petting; and at that stage we had stopped. Before discussing the possibility of going all the way, I suggested that we exchange a set of letters telling each other just what we thought of pre-marital intercourse, together with justifications for our positions. Our thoughts were identical.

The next weekend, as I took the commuter train to her home, I knew that we had reached the right decision, and was very happy that we had arrived at it independently. That night, after bidding good night to her parents, we retired to our separate wings of the house. I set my alarm for two thirty A.M., but didn't need it. At that hour I tiptoed through the house and gently slipped through her open, beckoning door. Neither of us slept that night, and with the dawnlight in the halls, I returned to my room. It had been the most overwhelming, the most beautiful experience of my life. I am convinced that nothing is more rewarding than making love, again and again, in every mood, in every state of physical strength, to a person with whom one achieves a complete psychological, cerebral, and physical rapport.

Sex was like a new poetic language; we were discovering new words and phrases and new combinations of old-word rhythms. The days between our weekend meetings became too long. My father ordinarily left his keys in his topcoat pocket. So I began borrowing his car late on Wednesday nights and driving the thirty miles to her home. Before retiring she would leave the front door ajar. I would park far down her driveway and, in stocking feet, climb the stairs to join her.

We always left her door open a fraction, to keep an ear cocked for noises in the rest of the house. One night her mother's door opened far down the hall. I quickly snatched up my effects from where they lay scattered all over the room and leaped into the closet. My heart was beating so furiously that I was sure it could be heard all through the house. Her mother stopped outside the room, swung open the door, and glanced around. But she noticed nothing amiss. After she closed the door again, I emerged from my hiding place behind the evening dresses. It took the better part of an hour for my heart to return to normal. After that it was no good that night; we were both too frightened.

Later, as I drove home at eighty miles an hour, I was stopped by the police. I had left home without my wallet, and so the police had to call my parents. When the officer told them that a young man, allegedly their son, had been apprehended in their car driving eighty miles an hour at five in the morning, my father would not believe it: he left the phone to check my bed, sure that I was in it. When he found that I was not, and that the car was really gone, he took a taxi to the station, settled with the police, and then wanted to settle with me. As an explanation I lamely said that I hadn't been able to sleep and so had gone for a drive. Strangely, he accepted this lie. Apparently no other explanation occurred to him.

But the combination of these two traumas spelled the end of the love affair. Apparently she was severely frightened by the whole situation, and saw continuing dangers in maintaining the liaison. Her ardor soon cooled, but mine did not. She deserted me, and I was badly shaken for over a year.

Beyond the loss of my virginity, the sharp, intense love affair had repercussions on my whole *Weltanschauung*. My parents are Roman Catholics, and since I was attending a nonsectarian school, they had insisted that I take religious instruction at a convent one afternoon a week. For one reason or another, however, I had not taken really intensive instruction in catechism, in preparation for confirmation, until I was about fifteen. But by then it had been too late; I hadn't been able to swallow the irrationalities and inconsistencies. When one is told to accept an incredible proposition on faith, the dogma becomes meaningless if one does not already *have* faith. The others at the catechism classes had been either converts, who were already blindly committed, or people planning to marry Catholics, who were completely bored. I, for my part, had raised objection after objection. When the dull young priest had consistently ignored my sincere reactions I had finally subsided, memorized the fatuous question-and-response answers, and had been duly confirmed in the Roman Catholic Church.

During my love affair I had not gone to Communion. This seemed necessary, for I sensed an unsolvable problem: I could not make a proper confession. I remember, about six weeks after the affair was over, kneeling in the neighborhood church for hours one afternoon prior to entering the confessional. It

had been a long time since I had confessed, and I was re-
viewing my sins of commission and omission. But I became
very confused when I thought of the recent affair. Though
it was over because the girl had ended it, I was still in love.
According to Catholic doctrine, I was obliged to confess my
sins of the flesh, say I was sorry for them, promise never to
commit them again, seek absolution, and perform penance.
But I could not! I was not sorry for having slept with the
girl: on the contrary, it was the most beautiful experience of
my life, the most rewarding, and the most satisfying. It was
the high point of my life up to that time and I could see no
wrong in it. I conceived of wrong quite simply: harming
others or one's self. That girl and I had not wronged each
other or ourselves; we had given each other an almost mystical
fulfillment, an experience of beauty and depth. It seemed
not wrong, but most right! And kneeling there in the church,
I knew that if she should have a change of heart and wish
to resume the relationship, I would be at her side as quickly
as I could join her. The Church said it was wrong, but I felt,
I *knew* it was right. I entered the confessional and ran through
my roll of minor transgressions. When I came to the real issue,
I stopped, unable to continue. Sure, in a few words I could
have sketched the affair to the priest, mumbled words of
repentance, and walked out absolved. But I could not abdi-
cate my judgment to Church authority, and would not lie to
God and myself. In the middle of the seance I rose from my
knees and left the confessional, outlawing myself from the
sacraments, and placing myself outside the body of the faithful by an act of will.

I came to the conclusion that the Roman Catholic Church
had failed me. It was not so much that Church doctrine did
not possess the truth, though that seemed to be the case, too,
but that it was irrelevant. It had created a problem for me
that had not previously existed, and then had failed to provide
an acceptable solution. From my catechism I remembered that

one was obliged to accept the entire body of Church dogma; the corollary is that denying any facet amounts to repudiating it all. I then denied all. Because I could not go to confession, I could not go to Communion. As all Roman Catholics are obliged to perform these ceremonies a specified number of times each year, I thenceforth began to consider myself outside the Church, as I still do.

At home, in the meantime, there was never any discussion of whether I would go to college or, for that matter, where. My father had graduated from a large land-grant university, but retained no ties to his school. He did not care where I went to college, and left the decision entirely in my hands. I chose Princeton, but really do not know why. Princeton had the reputation for a fine liberal-arts education, which was what I wanted; but more than that, I believe, I sought the aura of sophistication and relaxed good taste with which the slick-paper magazines endowed the university in their almost regular picture stories. Perhaps I was taken in by the "country club" tradition which still surrounded Princeton. Needless to say, I soon found this to have been an illusion, yet it did, I think, influence my choice. As I led my class scholastically, captained the football team, and was a "big wheel" (albeit in a small school), I felt none of the tension that pervades the air of prep schools in May when the best colleges send their acceptances. Before my application was submitted, I knew I would be accepted. Despite the urging of my Headmaster, I refused even to apply to another college; it seemed a waste of time.

Princeton provided no big obstacles my freshman year. As I had been well prepared in prep school, I found the work relatively easy. I tried out for the freshman football team, but after ten days discovered that I could not, or perhaps would not, match the speed and determination that characterized those who eventually composed the team; so I quit. I had been knocked out in one scrimmage, and used that as a pretext.

At my request, the university had quartered me in a room with three other freshmen, two of whom I hope to count as my friends for the rest of my life. My roommates and I did well in our courses and soon slipped into the habit of holding rather orgiastic drinking parties. It seemed at that time that the easiest way to meet classmates, and to meet the best men, was through all-night beer parties, sessions at the Annex, and blasts at the King's Inn. To a man, we all despised Commons where we were obliged to eat, and eagerly anticipated our entry into the club system (the social and dining facilities for juniors and seniors and Princeton's counterpart of the fraternity system).

I made no particular effort to cultivate the upperclassmen, assuming that the bicker (bidding) system would naturally filter me into the club of my choice. The club that I wanted was the one that had the reputation for the best bunch of drinkers and for the group of men who were the most amusingly vulgar. And it seemed to me, during the calling period, that the members of that club had also shown a very definite interest in me. Yet when the "Hour of Truth" arrived, they extended me no bid. I did receive an acceptance; but it was from another club further down the hierarchy. The club of my first choice had not wanted me! The whole experience was a trauma. For years, it seemed, I had had everything my way. That night, for the first time, I realized that just being me, and just doing as I wished, was not enough. Later that night I returned to my room and got very drunk.

At Princeton I have felt obliged to be a vociferous opponent of an irrational, anachronistic institution that has plagued freshmen and sophomores for decades: compulsory chapel. For the first two years of their university education, all undergraduates are required to attend religious services at least half the weeks of each term. They are told that

". . . It is a principle of the educational policy of Princeton that no man can be truly educated and at the same time religiously illiterate." Whereas the university justification for this compulsion implies that a reading knowledge of religion is part of the student's education, in fact the student is not obliged to *study* religion, but to *attend* services. (At least one is not required to worship!) Unquestionably, religion and religious controversy are part of the Western tradition and are legitimate subjects for study. But then, many other aspects of the Western tradition are studied at the university, and none of the others are the subject of compulsion. As a matter of fact, one may graduate with a Bachelor of Arts degree from Princeton without even taking a single course in English! (I know; I shall.)

Undoubtedly, the university has its reasons for requiring chapel attendance of its freshmen and sophomores. Whatever these reasons are, however, there is a much more fundamental reason why the whole operation *must* be a failure: sincere religion simply *cannot* be the subject of compulsion. Compulsion saps the very roots of religious enthusiasm. To some it is amusing, to some disgusting, to visit the Chapel balcony during Sunday services. There are three typical scenes: (1) a hungry student eating a sandwich; (2) another reading the newspapers; (3) the third so bored with the whole performance going on below that he is stretched out full length on one of the pews, snatching a nap before turning in his Chapel card. To those with sincere religious convictions who come to worship, the compulsion imposed on their fellows, and the latter's reaction to it, must be truly offensive. I consider any university obligation to participate in religious ceremonies an invasion of my personal rights and unjustifiable on any grounds. If Christianity cannot make a successful appeal to young men in competition with the myriad of other ideas to which they are exposed, then the religion has lost its vitality. If it has no intrinsic meaning to youth, as would seem to be implied by the apparent need for religious compulsion, then it is time that this be recognized.

I am convinced that the ethical code of Christianity encompasses the most exalted forms of human behavior, and I doubt that there will ever be any significant changes in its precepts. Its validity, however, rests on its intrinsic merits; it is destroyed by compulsion, for compulsion can destroy any ideational commitment, even patriotism. The merit of the ethical system of Jesus, moreover, transcends any question of his divinity. The ethic is the best; it matters not whether the promulgator was the Son of God or an egomaniacal Jewish rabble rouser. The validity of an argument is not affected by the condition of its author, though it may be best comprehended within the context of his society. It has been said that God is dead, that he was killed by the spinning jenny. More aptly, today, one might say that he was killed at Hiroshima. But whether killed by the Fords or the Tellers, the objective existence of God has been made irrelevant by the Industrial Revolution. Mankind is now dedicated not to the greater glory of God, but to the advancement of a this-worldly program of social justice and welfare. The Christian ethic no longer has the sanction of divine authorship; but it doesn't need it any more. The sanction for today's increasingly secularized Christianity is Mankind, or sometimes more narrowly, Social Justice. And that is sufficient as well as efficient.

In the junior year of Princeton one begins departmental concentration. I chose history. Why? Frankly, because it seemed slightly less tedious than the other disciplines. Like many other history majors, I had toyed with the idea of economics. Several courses in that field, however, convinced me that one would learn nothing of business by studying economics at Princeton; the courses seemed constructed around abstract politico-economic theory. The professors all seemed collectivists, at least to the extent of being committed to the increase of the sphere of governmental activity. Implicit in this is the notion that government has the right to apply compulsion; the prospect of such a study made me ill.

As a freshman I had had the privilege of taking a course lectured by an ancient professor with a prominent hearing aid and atrocious taste in clothes. He lectured too early in the morning, in the ugliest, coldest, most uncomfortable building on campus. The reading assignments were three times as long as those in other courses. Yet in 1952, approximately one quarter of the student body elected his course. He was magnificent. Apparently one of the last of the individualist professors, he lectured on twentieth-century war and revolution. I hope he gave the others, as he gave me, a faith in the power of the individual to advance human society in triumph over apparently insuperable odds. It was largely as a result of my contact with this professor that I elected to major in history. But I was disappointed, for the old gentleman in question retired that same year. Though there were historians on the faculty who had studied under him, none had assimilated his philosophy as I understood it. Most of them are pedantic, crushing bores, afraid of their own ideas and ashamed of their own individuality.

In the summer between my junior and senior years I was expelled from Princeton University. The Dean did not use precisely those words; his euphemism was ". . . required to withdraw. . . ." This came as a severe shock to me: the temperature, in the plains of Oklahoma during ROTC Artillery Officers' Summer Camp, was about 110 degrees. It was the day after the long Independence Day weekend, during which some friends and I had drunk through a rather exhausting four-day binge in Dallas. Fiercely hung over, I had been saddled that day with the rotating job of Battery Commander. I had been doing badly, and was pleased to see the envelope from the Dean's Office: I was expecting notification of my election to junior Phi Beta Kappa. Between the shimmering heat, my own interior climate, and the Dean's words, I felt like Camus's *Stranger*.

My career as regards discipline at Princeton had been a rather checkered one. I had been suspended twice: once as a freshman for drunkenness, and once as a junior for disobeying what I held to be an unfair and unjustified order of a university disciplinary official. During this second suspension, which occurred during the final weeks of my junior year, I was working on a ten-thousand-word history essay. Suspension or none, if I wanted credit for my year, the essay had to be completed. But how to complete the research for it, when my suspension included suspension of my Princeton library privileges? I finally resorted to the New York Public Library (and felt like Karl Marx working in the British Museum). Before I did, however, I had taken a book out of the Princeton library under a fictitious name. This in itself might have passed unnoticed. My undoing was that when I left Princeton for the summer I forgot to return the book, leaving it in my room. The university, apparently, called in a handwriting expert who matched the phony signature with the script of three thousand library users. My room was searched and the book was discovered there. Without summoning me for an explanation (what could I have said?), the Probation Board fired me. Despite my loss of university status, and my consequent ineligibility for the commission for which I was being trained by the army, I was still under military jurisdiction and had to finish summer camp. What tedium!

When the summer was over, I returned to Princeton for one final audience with the Dean. He suggested that I join the army and prove by honorable service to my country that my action had been a momentary mental aberration, and that I was worthy of a Princeton degree. I almost told him to take his ruddy university and ram it. But I did not, and did join the army, beginning the most unpleasant period of my life. A theologian once expounded the theory that hell for each individual is the continuation throughout eternity of the most unpleasant period of terrestrial existence. No intensification of the military system of America would be necessary to give me the worst conceivable hell. I developed an uncompromising, irrational hatred of all sergeants and officers, particularly colonels and generals. Even as I think of it now, my stomach turns and my mouth runs dry.

After the foul shock of basic training and a short stint in the hospital brought on by overexposure during winter maneuvers, I was sent to an army typing school. (Join the army. Learn a trade!) When my group "graduated" almost all the men were posted for overseas duty. Since I had studied French for over ten years and had majored in European History in college, I was sent to the Far East, in accordance with army logic. At the overseas replacement station I managed to wangle an appointment to an army school in Japan, thus vacating my orders to proceed to Korea.

I saw the world—from below the waterline of a rustbucket surely old enough to have served as Ben Hur's flagship. The accommodations were spacious—for the crew; the troops were stacked five deep like a deck of cards. The sheets of canvas on which the men were supposed to sleep were so close together that if a man sat on one instead of lying down, he sat on the chest of the man below. There was no ventilation, so the air below decks soon became a nauseous blend of sweat, vomit, and feet. There were a total of five chairs for three thousand men, and two of those were in the barbershop.

Arrival in Japan ended that fortnightmare. Entranced with the beauty of the land and the grace of the people, I entered upon the only period of military service that was less than agony. The school to which I was sent taught stenography, so for six hours a day I drew and later wrote shorthand. The teachers were adequate, the pace well modulated, and one never saw officers or NCO's. I began seeing a Japanese girl. After a complicated series of maneuvers she became my mistress. I was unable to arrange to live with her, but did spend many evenings and some nights with her. We achieved a degree of sexual compatibility that I had never previously experienced. There was no fear or tension, no unresolved conflict, no worry, and no strain in our relationship. It existed in a sort of void of civilization in which proximity and touch and sensuality were the whole of existence. Soon, however, the school term was over and I had to move to a new assignment. I fought for a job in Japan so that the girl could be with me; but, along with the rest of my class, I was sent to Korea. Later, in trips to Japan, I returned to her again, but it was never the same. For three months we had had something which, perhaps because of its very intensity, could not be picked up and laid down at the whim of the army.

I thought of marrying this Japanese girl. It seemed to me, however, that what we had was a physical communion, which might well not stand the strain of miscegenation. The qualities of subservience and self-abnegation in which Japanese women are trained make them good servants, but tend to subordinate the originality and mental stimulation I expect in a wife. Despite Michener, I am dubious of the prospects for success of cross-cultural marriages. But the situation catalyzed my thoughts on marriage.

As economic forces are the basis of social order to a Marxist, on which religion, politics, etc., rest as superstructure, so to me is sexual compatibility the foundation and *sine qua non* of marriage. It is so basic that without it marriage is inconceivable. In addition, I would seek in a wife a great many values, none of which, however, is particularly rare. Most simply, I would say I desire a woman in whom I would find, as she would in me, a sense of completeness, a mystical sense of new unity, a sort of transcendence of self, that is presently lacking in me.

Since being posted to Korea meant my separation from

the girl to whom I had become so attached, I hated the place even before I got there. Upon arrival I found that I was not needed; but there is no return from Korea until one's sentence is served. The country functions as a vast penitentiary, or perhaps workhouse, of infinite degradation and inhumanity for over fifty thousand innocent Americans. All over the world, the spectre of Korea is used by the American Army as a threat, as the last legal torture employed to break an innocent man.

Korea is called the Land of the Morning Calm. More aptly, it should be called the Land of the Pervading Stench. The land is ugly and unkempt. The cities are filthy havens of thieves and prostitutes. The people are sly and untrustworthy and exude the most offensive odor imaginable. The latter is the first thing one notices; it is said to come from eating a popular food known as *kimshee,* a particularly vile dish of rotten cabbage, peppers, garlic, and decomposed raw fish. This is supplemented by a national resistance to cleanliness that would warm the heart of Bathless Groggins. Every decent quality of the Japanese is inverted in the Koreans. They are led by an ancient Fascist whom the United States supports (though with some military reservations). The last Presidential election was cute: Mr. Shin, Syngman Rhee's liberal opponent, died under mysterious circumstances a few days prior to the election. This was particularly fortunate for the ruling gang, for even though dead, and his death widely publicized, Mr. Shin polled more votes in the country's most important province than did the living Mr. Rhee. The United States supports this government with almost five hundred million dollars yearly. A popular estimate among American administrators in Korea is that some ten per cent of that amount is lost through Korean graft and supervised theft.

But for most of the American troops in Korea these factors are not important; their concern is bare existence. American forces in Korea are probably the worst fed, clothed, and housed of all American forces anywhere in the world. Typical is the housing situation. It was estimated that in the winter of 1955–56, the sixth winter in which Americans occupied Korea in force, and three years after the end of the "conflict," forty per cent of the troops were still living in tents. When the rainy season comes, they live in mud to their knees. The troops just south of the DMZ (the demilitarized zone separating Communist from American forces) are treated the worst of all. They spend their days running up and down hills. At night when they return "home" there is usually no electricity. For showers they must walk miles, or, if lucky, ride in clouds of dust that make bathing almost pointless. In freezing weather they shave in ice water. During the unbelievably cold winter nights regulations require that the small stoves in the tents be turned off. There are so few movies that to see one it is necessary to stand in line often for hours. There are almost no chairs for the troops. Eight months of the year all local restaurants and bars are off limits. American soldiers are not permitted to bring their wives and children to Korea (one general, however, did live with *his* family).

Korea contains the fifty thousand loneliest men in the world. Such meagre recreational facilities as do exist are hopelessly overcrowded. Most enlisted men are not permitted to purchase bottled liquor, though in some areas they may buy a drink across an army bar. There is not a single pleasure that would bring a ray of light into the lives of the men in Korea. All count the days until they emerge from their prison. The dearth of wholesome recreation, or even distraction, is reflected in the regular patronage of prostitutes by tens of thousands of officers and men who would not consider such a thing in a normal life. Though the army is understandably vague about this, one incredible statistic was quoted to me: sixty per cent of the men who leave Korea have had one or more cases of venereal disease there.

Shortly after I arrived in Korea I was contacted by the director of a Korean school. (How he obtained my name is still a mystery.) I was asked to teach English to Koreans during my free time at night. The class ranged in age from twelve to seventy, male and female. They were all pathetically eager to learn English—as they had probably been eager to learn Japanese during their occupation. Respecting their intense desire to learn both the language and customs of the United States, I taught myself how to teach. This daily contact with a poor and ignorant people was usually depressing, but I felt I was doing something. This continued for some months until the pressure of my military job made it impossible to schedule classes. One of my students was a Korean major general. At his request I tutored him privately in his home. As he had a tape recorder I was able to employ some of the audio technique I had learned studying French at Princeton. We worked together for over a year, and his progress was quite gratifying. From him I learned something of Korean culture—and a good bit about local politics.

My regular army job, in the meantime, was as stenographer in the office of the Chief of Staff, a two-star general. I soon grew to hate my boss and so had to develop the strongest self-discipline. I was in daily contact with a man whom I could not stand, and who had absolute power over me. Quite literally, I lived and could have died at his whim. I was polite—much more so than he. West Point seems to produce a plethora of boors. I think I fooled him. But as I hated him, I began hating the army, and ended up by hating those who organized and condoned the whole system. And then I became angry with myself for what the whole experience was doing to me. But it all stayed inside. I played their game because I had to, and I was never officially or unofficially reprimanded or punished. And I think I left that hell almost a sane man. But it was several months after leaving that despicable peninsula before I could discuss it rationally.

One of the residues of my army experience in Korea was an abhorrence of regularized office jobs that now colors my plans for the future. I never want to sit behind a desk again, never want to live the vacant life that would permit, would glorify that total commitment to the job which seems to be a precondition for success in commerce as well as in the military. Success for me would mean a job that I could leave after eight hours and that would provide for self-fulfillment within a framework of inconspicuous luxury.

Such a "low" level of ambition inevitably raises the question of security. As at present I am foundering among sincere, irrational antipathies, I can only think of security in broad generalities: it is to be found in creating a life that in some sense partakes of popularly approved values, and contributes to socially approved goals. And this is the problem: if one does not conform to the values and subscribe to the goals, one will have no security. I feel myself slipping into this position and recognize that I must accept the consequences. I cannot work or think, or act or live as a member of a collective; thus I am outside the stream of mid-twentieth-century America. I cannot beat them (and really have no desire to), and will not join them. I must abjure any claim to status or prestige. Both are exterior to the life of the individual, are institutionalized reflections of social approbation. They exist exterior to the individual as functions not of merit or competence, but of successful conformity. They are the new Holy Grail; but their conscious quest is the prostitution of the soul, the denial of the birthright of the free individual.

What is that birthright? Freedom to develop the self according to its *own* capacities. The avenue of that development, and incidentally the hope of humanity, is education. The salvation of humanity is not God—He has not helped anybody since He forsook His Son on the cross—but bootstrap self-help and education.

With these thoughts in mind I returned to Princeton for my final year. Readjustment to civilian and academic life after two years of the tyranny and stagnation of the service was not easy. Before resuming my education, I had about a week at home. My friends handled me gently. My parents had dismissed as "normal gripes" the comments I had addressed to them in letters, and were somewhat lacking in understanding of my bitterness. But then, they have always been lacking in understanding. Princeton appeared much the same—the students a bit younger, the lectures duller and less pertinent to reality, and the restrictions of the administration even more ridiculous than before. Almost all of my friends had graduated. Their absence, however, had for me a salutary effect. It was no longer necessary to indulge in the constant creation of ideas and stunts of imaginative vulgarity to maintain a reputation for "bad news"—one of my previous avocations. It was no longer necessary to go on the unwanted drinking sprees to keep friends company. I could drink when *I* felt the desire.

I soon became completely wrapped up in writing a thesis for the History Department. To my knowledge, Princeton is the only university that requires both a senior thesis and comprehensive departmental examinations for a bachelor's degree. At first I dreaded the prospect of a twenty-five-thousand-word paper written from research into primary source materials. Once into the actual work, however, I became fascinated. Now that it is completed and handed in, I actually treasure the hundreds of hours I devoted to researching and writing my thesis. It was the most rewarding educational experience of my Princeton career. I would go so far as to say that those who miss such an experience have been shortchanged in their education.

Now that I am rapidly approaching the end of my senior year at Princeton, I must inevitably think of the future. I am still unsettled in my plans, but I know some things I do *not* want. I do not want to have anything to do with the army. Unpatriotic as it may seem, unless the United States were attacked, it would take a court order and an armed platoon of soldiers to get me in again. I will not accept regimentation or compulsion, whether in the army or anywhere else. The only control I respect is that which is self-imposed. I do not want an ordered life, regularity, or their concomitant responsibilities. My continuing problem, as I see it, is to find my identity, to find my place in a society which demands a total commitment that I cannot give. I believe in the sovereign individual, and feel myself at bay.

The two poles of self-conscious bohemianism and cynical conformity are both repellent. I have had job interviews, but I do not want to sell soap. One day I think I might want to study business administration at graduate school; another day I want to go to Paris and study existentialism, or to Heidelberg or Oxford. When I graduate, I can study two more years on the Korean GI Bill, and it seems foolish to pass up the opportunity. Sometimes I feel like going to Florida or Acapulco to work as a water-ski instructor or a deck hand on a tourist fishing boat.

But this I do want: to live in freedom, unrestricted by exterior compulsion. I want my contribution to life to be a living testimonial that individual freedom is compatible with the welfare and progress of society.

TO ATTAIN SIGNIFICANCE

EACH MAN HAS A DESIRE TO ASSERT HIMSELF in some meaningful way, to act so that he will express the importance of his individuality. Society offers him a limited number of possible lives, and he must attempt to evaluate these and to choose from among them. Some choose business or a profession, others politics or family, but even the uneducated factory worker devotes himself to his new car or brags to his fellows about his adventures because he wants to attain significance.

I have been fortunate. Being able to attend Princeton opens up a great many alternatives, while the education itself should help one to make decisions wisely. Until recently, however, two considerations have made me hesitant in my attempts to plan for the future. The processes of our society, in the first place, force me to choose my vocation at a time when I am poorly equipped to do so. Still immature, only twenty-one, I am yet obliged to make major decisions, decisions which will drastically affect my whole life. This is doubly unfortunate, because I am still ignorant of the true nature of the alternatives I am considering. Every senior at Princeton is in this position, and while we have been taught the "liberal arts," few of us are capable of judging accurately the alternatives open to us. Perhaps it is not Princeton's responsibility to prepare us to make this important decision more knowledgeably, but I fear that many of its graduates will discover that they have become misfits, that they are no longer suited to the careers they picked as younger men.

Secondly, even before one can choose between poorly understood alternatives, one must dig deeply into oneself. Each of us who wishes to assert himself significantly has first to discover what constitutes his "self." He must root out and re-evaluate his most basic desires and beliefs so that he can plan a future which will most adequately give expression to his nature. For the past two years I have been trying to unravel my own thoughts and emotions, and, although this process has caused me to be unduly confused and self-conscious, it has brought me to a new level of self-evaluation (from which I must begin again each day). Through trying to know myself I should also be able to make truer and freer decisions, because self-awareness lifts men above the animals and some men above others.

I found it necessary to re-examine my past. Because it had implanted in my mind most of my basic emotions, I reasoned, these latter could not be evaluated apart from the perspective it affords. Perhaps the study of my background would, therefore, enable me to distinguish my biases from my true beliefs. It is, at any rate, a past filled with the tensions of insecurity. As far back as I can remember, the little stability my family was able to maintain was precarious. We were constantly moving from place to place, trying to become adjusted to new towns and new people and, it seemed, moving on again just as some semblance of composure was being reached. Within the family, too, there was disorder. My father was Irish, my mother a Jew. They originated from completely antipodal cultural and ideological climates, and the growing resentment which we sensed between them gave us children cause for alarm.

We knew that the real blame for our parents' conflict lay with our father. At the time, both I and the older of my two sisters hated him, but now, when we can think of him without looking back at those times, we only pity him. I shall attempt to describe my father and his actions, because the reaction against his nature is basic to mine.

To most people he appeared to be a typical small-town boy out to make good in the city; but the small town he came from was predominantly ignorant and amoral, and he, in turn, was ready to use any means available to "make good." At his best, he was merely a hypocrite, assuming whatever guise seemed suitable for a particular situation—he used to practice smiling before a mirror. At his worst, he was dishonest, and he continually turned against and used the very people who had given him love and support. His shallow opportunism was revealed most clearly in his family life. When he and my mother had been married only a few days, he admitted readily that he didn't love her, that she was just a "nice girl" whose family he hoped would help him financially. Each time my mother became pregnant he advocated an abortion; it was only her perseverance which barely succeeded in preventing my own life from being cut off before its beginning. Finally my father was unfaithful to my mother. He committed adultery with a married woman—whom he later also left—and used her love to help him in his business ventures.

My mother's assumptions, on the other hand, and the actions in which they were expressed were completely opposed to my father's, and her presence has taught me, by precept and example, the principles in which I now believe. Finally unwilling to submit to his degradations any longer, she divorced my father; and, having done the right thing, she was prepared to accept the inevitable consequences. For the last five years she has guided the family and provided its financial support. With courage and strength and love she has fought to insure her children's happiness, sacrificing herself so that we should never be deprived by her decision to break from my father.

My own convictions have been heavily influenced by my attitudes towards my parents. I find myself almost revelling in the ugliness of my father's nature because that ugliness is a constant justification of my own complete reaction against all the beliefs and desires he represents to me. Even as I wrote of him above, I understood more clearly how the negation of him has shaped my thinking. My complete approbation of my mother's character, however, and my love for her have given me a more positive approach to life and its problems. On two counts, though, it is unfortunate that my acceptance of the principles represented by my mother has been influenced so strongly by the emotional content of my past. My convictions have tended sometimes to become irrational biases, so that I criticize not only opportunism and the hunger for money but also the slightest signs of ambition, whether they be healthy or not. Similarly, I resent even the mildest forms of hypocrisy, some of which are necessary for social intercourse. And secondly, the emotional formation of uncompromising values has led me to condemn myself and all others who cannot measure up to my table of values. I am often tormented by my own feelings of guilt, and at other times I censure the people around me so absolutistically that I become positively self-righteous.

This attitude has been strengthened by a facet of my past which I have already mentioned. Because my family was constantly moving from place to place, I usually found myself outside the social groups formed by people my own age. For years, it seemed, life was a long struggle to gain acceptance; finally, as I grew up, I abandoned this struggle and more and more remained an outsider by choice. From the almost unhealthy vantage point which my detachment gave me, I began to judge and condemn the ways of my contemporaries. Sometimes I judged correctly, other times not; but my viewpoint remained artificial, I think, until my second year at college.

These, then, are the aspects of my past which have been important in forming my thinking. Recognizing them has freed me of them in so far as I can honestly re-evaluate the convictions to which they have given rise. This is true because each man is capable of internalizing his beliefs, of converting them into assumptions which can effectively guide his life; he is the aimless product of his prenatal temperament only if he fails to achieve self-awareness. Recently I have reassessed the prejudices which supported my thoughts, and, while most of my beliefs held true, their basis in my mind is more reliable than it was before.

I have come to think that life is a tremendous gift, a short but potentially valuable release from the anonymity of nonlife; and I look on it as a chance to prove or disprove myself. It is possible to squander this gift aimlessly as my father did; the lack of love which he evinced and his opportunism, hypocrisy, and disloyalty are among the qualities which presage a wasted, meaningless life. Each man must consciously seek for worth-while principles, and he should find symmetry and order by squaring his actions with his beliefs. I do not want to waste my life and to indicate, by my own futility and worthlessness, the emptiness of human life itself. Each person who denies his responsibility to be fully and valuably human detracts from the dignity of the human status, which is not only the sum of all of us but also the extension of each individual.

Measuring the Princeton undergraduate in this light, I have been disappointed, but I suppose that my "idealism" will always be prone to disappointment. Even among Princeton boys, the cream of the nation, there is much wasted potential. Many of them, in their anxiety to fit into patterns of thought and action which their predecessors established, ignore completely what should be their real concerns, while others possess admirable principles which, however, are often crowded out by extraneous concerns. In the latter category, for example, I place many of the "do-gooders" whom we all know. We find among them the undergraduate "pusher" who exercises his embryonic political ambitions by asserting his authority over a mimeograph machine and a loyal cohort of freshmen. The "religionist" is another who falsifies good intentions. Many of them claim to be capable of determining the will of God in any altercation, but their preoccupation with their own souls tends to make them ignore their human responsibilities. Others of this group are completely hypocritical to their professed beliefs.

At Princeton, also, there is a small minority of people who have only the convictions dictated by self-interest and whose rapacity is animal-like. As a freshman I heard an upperclassman assert that "I got into this world only to get what I could out of it," and I later found out that this boy did not stand alone. Then there is a somewhat larger group of boys here whose minds seem to dwell in a state of limbo. They are fittingly called "shallow tweeds," and I suppose that the counterpart to this type can be found in any school or society. Digging below their superficial personalities, one is constantly astonished to find a complete void. Their minds are truly little more than hollow containers used for collecting at face value all the disconnected ideas and socially appropriate lingo which float through the Princeton atmosphere. It is to this group that "conformity" can be really dangerous. Necessary and valuable in all societies, conformity can be a poisonous thing to those whose weak and pliable personalities are completely susceptible to external influences. At Princeton, the willing initiate is taught that self-interest and disloyalty are valuable qualities, and he soon becomes proficient at varying his beliefs and purported commitments to suit the social situation at hand. Although few of them really believe that they are in this world only for what they can get out of it, they are all too ready to accept the external forms of behavior and emotions which could be expected to accompany this belief. Most of them seem anxious to achieve indifference to other people and to the emotions and bonds which tie people together. For many of them love between the sexes becomes no more than pointless promiscuity in which their love-partners are simply useful and enjoyable objects.

I have been told that the attitudes with which these boys disguise themselves are really harmless, that they themselves see through them already, and that they are still young and resilient enough to reassert their real selves again. It may be true that they are critical of the values which they pretend temporarily to have accepted, but this fact itself would imply to me a strong and disturbing ethical relativism. I seriously doubt that all of these boys will, in the future, be able to disengage themselves from their social involvements long enough to formulate and establish a set of genuine convictions which will give them a basis for integrity and a worth-while life. The real point is that they are among the most intelligent people in the country and will someday be among its leaders; as such they should be the men most capable of rejecting opportunistic conforming.

That ignorant people should be easily misguided and carried along by the tide of social pressure is not surprising; but I find it terrible that on the "enlightened," liberal campus of Princeton cultural and racial prejudice, for example, should prevail to the extent that it does. Here, one would think, the Jew's desperate need to overcome social antipathy would be mitigated and he would be able to assume that he was on a par with others. This is not the case, however, and the Jew's plight stands out very dramatically, for instance, in Princeton's much-discussed club hierarchy.

Coming from mixed parents myself, I have always been sympathetic with the unfortunate position of minority groups in this country, although I myself have not suffered from being Jewish since my childhood. In this country the Negro, for instance, is born into the knowledge that his is a second-rate race. Society teaches him to assume this. The white people control the country, and a Negro politician is regarded as an oddity. History has been shaped by the whites, and cultural tastes depend on their likes and dislikes. Each time a Negro attends a movie or watches television he learns anew that this is a white man's world, that in it the Negro is a problem child or a joke, a Rochester. The psychologist would tell us that each Negro inherits an inferiority complex and that much of his time is preoccupied with overcompensation. The Negro is generally loud, immoral, and violent because he is looking for ways to assert himself and his significance in the face of a society which assumes his inferiority. The Jew, too, is treated either as a problem or a joke, but he will not allow his irrational longing for expression to be stifled. He devotes himself to his family or his business and exudes an energy and enthusiasm which our society finds distasteful. My point, of course, is that these races can never become "acceptable" until they have been accepted. They will exhibit some of the symptoms of inferiority for as long as they are treated as inferiors, and the responsibility for giving them self-respect lies with society.

It would seem that even at Princeton people are not prepared to accept this responsibility and to give each person the respect due him. The Jews here (there are virtually no Negroes despite Princeton's purported liberalism) are forced to seek out one another for solace. They "grind" harder because they want to express themselves in some way and to overcome their insecurity by obtaining good jobs once they have graduated. It is pitiful to see many of the Jews try to gain acceptance by assuming the traditional "Ivy" characteristics. I have always sympathized with the bewilderment and loneliness of the incoming Jewish freshmen, because I remember clearly the unhappiness I experienced myself when I first entered the strange, even alien, Princeton atmosphere.

I have allowed myself to exaggerate the evils of the Princeton campus, primarily because I am disappointed with some of its people. Were there not so much valuable potential going to waste here, the disappointment would not be so great. The picture is probably not as bleak as I paint it, but I am moved to criticize severely by the feeling that many essentially good people are being dishonest to themselves, are doing things they do not really want to do, and are repressing spontaneously good emotions. It is not Princeton, I should add, which is at fault here. Despite the indifference of many of the faculty towards undergraduates, the university succeeds in offering its students a rich and sound education. If the student participates creatively in the classes and other activities available here, he can profit immensely from his four years.

The real fault for the failings of some of our generation lies with its parents. Schools can make ideals available to their students and can even encourage them to accept the responsibilities which come with maturity. Only within the family group, however, can the young person find the care and affection with which he must be taught to respect himself and other people. The family must impart to him, in other words, the qualities which lead him into genuine human maturity. Today, however, parental care and affection are not so strong as they once were, and the entire responsibility for educating the young is more and more being conferred on professionals. Very often, in fact, a boy is sent to prep school simply because there is no place for him within the home or because the home itself has been split apart. A friend of mine calculated that more than forty-five per cent of the boys in his graduating class at one of the country's top prep schools came from families in which the parents were divorced or separated. The family no longer exemplifies for its progeny the convictions and emotions which strengthen character and human solidarity.

In setting down all these thoughts and reactions, I have, of course, also revealed, at least implicitly, a good deal about myself. What I personally desire above all else is a life which will be creative, which will leave behind it some permanent and positive result in surrounding lives. The vocation which, after much doubt and soul-searching, I have chosen to enable me to achieve this goal in life is that of teaching.

The public-high-school system, in which I plan to teach, has always been and is becoming increasingly important in the country's educational structure. The high-school years are, in many respects, the most crucial of the young person's formative years. Many of the students are obliged to choose their life's work shortly after leaving high school; this is even true of many who go on to college studies. Prospective engineers and businessmen, for instance, begin specialized training as soon as they enter college, while even the liberal-arts students are expected to select their field of learning, their "major," by the second college year. It is essential, therefore, that the high schools arouse as many interests as possible in their "college-prep" students and mold their capacities for judgment. Each of these high-school graduates should begin at an early date to consider the advantages and qualities of the vocations in which they might be interested.

It is the job of the secondary school, also, to prepare its students for college simply by training them in the techniques of reading, writing, and thinking. I mention this because I believe that the high schools have been doing an inadequate job in this regard. Witness their procedure in teaching the young person to read with perception and understanding. Only the most imaginative teachers seem able to resist relying on the old standbys—*A Tale of Two Cities*, *Silas Marner*, and *The Return of the Native*. Though these may be great literature, they are not, at least in my experience, suited to arouse the enthusiasm of high-school-age students. I myself read the Dickens book three times, under three different teachers, until I was thoroughly bored with it. Other teachers use poorly written and uninspired adventure stories, such as Owen Wister's *The Virginian*, which may stimulate the young minds but teach them nothing. The dispirited question-and-answer analyses with which my own teachers used to accompany our readings not only taught us little about the art of reading but caused many of us to become devoted anti-intellectuals.

Because the number of college-age students is rising rapidly from year to year, it will not be too long before many more people will be able to acquire only a high-school education. It is the education of these "limited" students, those who will not go on with their formal education, that is or should be the high school's primary responsibility. The secondary school will give them their final formal guidance towards mature citizenship and participation in the community, and they must therefore be given the type of education which will stimulate their capacities to appraise and formulate their own goals and values. I am particularly interested in helping this type of student to think creatively and responsibly.

The goals which I have set forth for the secondary schools are difficult to attain, and the individual teacher, aside from his being underpaid, is liable to disillusionment and disappointment. As a result, the profession of public-high-school teacher attracts many too many incompetents to whom the future of the country should not be entrusted. The graduates of the better colleges can hardly be expected to ignore the many lucrative alternative career opportunities which are open to them when they know that teachers' salaries barely afford subsistence.

In my own case, the disadvantages of the teaching profession were aggravated by personal circumstances. Two years ago I met, fell in love with, and asked to marry a girl whose parents have money and means. The consequences of this are obvious. During the entire time in which I have been considering the possibility of teaching, I have been faced with the almost immediate prospect of having to support a wife and a family. The vocation and the family seemed for a long time to be irreconcilable. My future wife's parents, moreover, had worked to give their family financial security and a life of comparative luxury and ease. By choosing a vocation which offered such small financial benefits, I would be nullifying, in effect, much of their effort and would be departing from a way of life to which my wife would have been accustomed. I fear that I may yet be sorry for believing that all these considerations can be overcome, but I have decided, nevertheless, that I shall enter the teaching profession. The financial remuneration will at first be inadequate, but I hope to increase it by working in the summers and, as the years pass, by obtaining more responsible positions within the school system. I shall always know, at any rate, that the ends in view are valuable and well worth the effort needed to surmount whatever obstacles I encounter.

As the future approaches, it becomes obvious that education will be increasingly important in this country. New technological advances will require more and better high-school-trained people. The schools must, at the same time, teach their graduates how to pass their increased leisure time profitably and constructively. And education must render its greatest service of all, in my opinion, in preparing people—internationally as well as domestically—to overcome the pressures of ignorance, pride, and misunderstanding which stand in the way of better and more peaceful and co-operative human relationships.

The reason for my faith in education as an instrument to support the universal goal of co-operation and peace is that I believe that man everywhere, as a human being, has a spiritual capacity to which education can appeal. It is this spiritual capacity which enables man, at least potentially, to view the world in its proper perspective and to resolve his inner conflicts as well as those which arise between him and his fellows.

I believe, also, that there is something eternal which is the basis of all spirituality, values, and meaning. I call this eternal being God because this word implies fatherhood, guidance, and loving goodness. My belief is not complete. Often

I wonder how my reason could be so blinded as to accept the notion of God; but more often my nature spontaneously needs and appeals to some eternal, immutable source of wisdom and authority. I know that man can be good without God and that most men are satisfied to live without Him, but I, at least, have a deep and personal knowledge of His necessity. Without Him life would be nothing, chaotic, and purposeless. My own life would be a lie and all my aspirations futile.

IN DEFENSE OF IDENTITY

SINCE EARLY CHILDHOOD THREE QUALITIES have been impressed upon me as the route to the fullest realization of a man's potential: keenness of mind, unimpeachable integrity, and a stability and balance in one's approach to any problem. The lessons of my home have been especially strong in molding in me a pattern that inextricably intertwines each of these elements and that teaches that without the others any one is useless.

The attitudes reflected in this ethic, and the outlooks to which it gives rise, are founded on the coexistence of contradictories implied in my background. The ultimate irreconcilability of mutual antagonisms, and the constant restructuring of priorities that this involves, have taught me to scorn the man who pretends to absolute truth, and to live peaceably with the inevitability of frustration and irresolution.

I have been raised in a home that is a fusion of the obscurantism of the past and the enlightenment of the present. A profound religious commitment is held as deeply as the devotion to scientific principles in the secular realm. Dispassionate reason reigns in its own sphere even as emotion and sentimentality hold sway in another. Progressiveness and traditionalism are each influential within their own circumscribed limits.

Rather than a source of weakness or irresponsibility, I see in the coexistence of the contradictories reflected in my home

147

environment a source of dynamism and strength. For as I mature, and as my powers of analysis and reason develop, I discover that consistency is not the hallmark of human order in the universe. The teaching of the sage, "to everything there is a season and a time to every purpose under the heavens," assumes greater meaning and significance as I begin to recognize more clearly that the cult of logic and precision of reason has not only its limitations and frustrations but its distortions of truth as well. Though I admire the supremely logical mind to the extreme, I have recently found, on the first level, that the realm of reason and analysis is like everything else, circumscribed. It is precisely the unexpected and the inconsistent that give life its peculiar spontaneity and joy.

On a more sophisticated plane, the preoccupation of the young generations of this century with reasoned analysis, and their anxiety to pursue to the limit the implications of their scientific understanding of any problem or situation, can be valuable as academic exercise and abstract game. The discovery of the viability of reason, however, is all too often frequently followed by a cult which glorifies it as an omniscient and unlimited tool. Though I applaud any effort to develop this highest capacity of the human personality, its use must be limited by a recognition that it represents but one facet of the complexity of our minds. Even less dramatic indications than the ultimate finiteness of human comprehension may be cited as evidence that there is a point beyond which unfettered reason cannot go if we are to maintain some semblance of reality and happiness.

As with all other standards, it is reasonable to expect that the intellectually aware *nouveaux riches* will be infatuated with the powers of their toy to the extent that they will see no limitation on its use or its effectiveness. Part of the process of maturing, I think, is a recognition that, though rigid, undeviating standards, allowing no compromise with pre-established principle, are admirable in the young and the sweetly naïve, they are painful and dangerous features of an adult personality. A child, in everything, learns by relying on extremes and absolutes, whether in morality or faith. As he develops, however, he must surrender his constant and obsessive preoccupation with consistency in all thought and action.

I find this brief challenged by many of my fellows. In the throes of adolescent rebellion, they insist that there is only one method to truth, that there can be but one right, and that the weight of tradition is meaningless when it appears to obstruct the road to the ultimate implication of any "reasoned" principle or idea. Though I recognize that tradition can indeed be used merely as a brake on change, the pattern of man's accumulated knowledge and experience appears to me to argue irrefutably that the burden of proof rests on those who seek to innovate or destroy. Thus, a man must be thoroughly schooled in the very traditions whose alteration he advocates before he can presume to demand that he be respected and heard.

Significantly enough, I think, the historical pattern suggested by the combined experience of men with insight into the problems of the society in any discipline supports the thesis that he who follows this path is, more often than not, not rendered impotent by the majesty of the information over which he gains control. The result, rather, is a self-confidence and sober, restrained respect for the wisdom of his predecessors that affords him that discrimination and maturity of judgment that enables one to retain what is of value and discard that which errs.

I began this essay by positing three great values under whose influence I have been raised. I have devoted some attention to the third because it is the most elusive, the most subjective, and the most frequently neglected and disparaged. Less easily recognized than the value of a keen mind and a sense of decency and fair play is the importance of the mental context and frame of reference in one's approach to any of the myriad of decisions that a human being is constantly called upon to make.

Man is simultaneously a social and an individual animal. His training and orientation must point in the direction of both of these emphases. Even a man whose mind is as alert and clear as can ever be expected, and whose abstract standards of conduct are as pure as can humanly be attained—even such a man can easily dissipate his ability and potential unless the attitude and discipline that he brings to any situation is fitting and appropriate. Certainly the objective of education must be to develop insofar as possible latent powers of reason and intellect. Yet, a concomitant, if not a fundament, of this goal must be a training that focuses attention on the sharp definition of a man's objectives on any occasion, and that teaches discrimination and judgment in the selection of relevancies.

A vital aspect of the cultural and intellectual traditions in which I have been raised has been, I am convinced, the stress placed on this quality that I alternately call good taste, discretion, propriety, and intellectual discipline. It is the ability to construct a hierarchy of values, to determine from among the many influences to which one is constantly subjected, those most worthy of attention in the first instance. An educational institution or training that is devoted to the highest development of its product must consciously strive to prepare the student to make independent value judgments, to undertake independent analysis, in short, to lead an independently thoughtful and reasoned life.

I see in the realization of this goal one of the great assets of a Princeton education. Young men from a wide variety of backgrounds and home environments, where different qualities of an individual have been stressed and taught, are banded together in a close and intimate relationship on a university campus. Under the encouragement of a residential situation, persons with markedly different outlooks are confronted in a continuing and thoroughgoing manner with value systems and patterns of thought and action of a dramatically different character.

Those who arrive at college with the advantage of a training and background which has emphasized a specific standard of intellect and conduct are subjected to the rigor of a challenge to previously unquestioned criteria. Though in the resultant emotional conflict with the attractive dominant social ethic of superficial frivolity a man may assume the surface signs of protective coloration, he frequently emerges the stronger for his bout with values he knows to be empty and uninspiring. Thus, for short periods a man may succumb to the temptation to abjure any seriousness of purpose or intent whatever. As he matures emotionally and intellectually under the pressures of time and a demanding academic discipline, however, he forges for the first time an independent ethic that combines the best in his home tradition with a capacity to adapt and reorder his own value system under the exigencies of any one moment or situation.

The worth of a Princeton education, I am convinced, does not make its greatest impact on an individual until he has gained the perspective which distance and reflection can afford. The divergent and often conflicting values to which he has been exposed fall into sharper relief, and allow the mind formally trained for intelligent judgment and selection to make, in a quiet and dignified fashion, that decision that marks the threshold to maturity and the turning point to a useful life.

The myriad of experiences of four years of growing up in the company of one's fellows pass in kaleidoscopic fashion before the mirror of one's mind. Drunken bouts at local taverns, the shocking presumptuousness of "social selectivity," the inspiration of a dedicated teacher, the overwhelming reward of serious conversation and thought, are some of the sensations which one has known perhaps once and for all during the freedom of youth. Now they all assume a clearly understood relevance and importance. The student of yesterday returns to the sobriety of the home he had temporarily left behind and regards with no more than wistful reminiscence much of his undergraduate experience. Yet, he can be grateful to the institution that encouraged him to combine abstraction with practicality, and that trained him to distinguish those elements of his experience that he will appropriate as part of his own ethic and standard.

For nearly everyone, though surely less so for some than others, Princeton represents a wonderful, sustained four-year high pitch of excitement on every level. It encourages, gently in some instances, far less so in others, each of its students to expand his area of interest, to widen his horizons so that insofar as possible his personality will become a microcosm of all of the various experiences to which a human being in our society is exposed. It sees its function as extending beyond the world of the classroom, and in its application of the idea, interestingly enough, incurs the scorn of educational purists and the antagonism of resentful students as well.

The recognition by the university that her responsibility for education cannot be restricted to the classroom alone accounts for her insistence that her charges live as part of a university community, and that they know, even if they should ultimately choose to reject, the values and standards of the society which she reflects.

Some may argue, with some justification, that a willingness to accept this thesis applauding the totality of a Princeton educational experience marks a compromise with the purity of the university idea. I would argue, rather, as one who proposes to associate himself professionally with a college, that it realistically modifies the medieval university conception to which it is no longer merely quaint or unrealistic, but indeed dangerous, to cling.

A college can no longer hope for a product who will be

able to command with a flick of his concentration the complexities of information in all of the diverse streams of accumulated knowledge. To try to approach this ideal in four years, without any guiding idea that envisions adequate and satisfactory compensations and rationalizations for the college experience which inevitably falls short of it, is a sign of folly and incompetence.

Undergraduate training today must hope to mold a specific character of mind: one capable of remaining afloat in the sea of the staggering burden of fact and intricacy in a wide variety of disciplines. What some cynically call the superficiality of a Princeton or liberal education I see as its very source of strength. In a real sense, if the arrogance of the statement may be indulged, Princeton and her sister institutions are training future presidents of General Motors. That is to say, only incidentally does she produce qualified technicians in any specific field, be it medicine, engineering, or the law. Her real value to the community lies in her reasoned aspiration that her students will develop under her careful guidance qualities of mind that will enable them to deal competently with large accumulations of information and "technicalia." With a presumptuousness that might offend and shock the specialist, this bachelor of the arts is able to penetrate the minutiae of fact and statistic, to superimpose a forest on trees, to apply powers of broad conceptual understanding to any given situation or circumstance.

Surely the same capacity that this individual brings to professional problems he can apply with equal validity to his personal life and ethic. The final vindication of this modern educational idea of which I have been speaking lies in the fact that it trains for the totality of life. For the same qualities of mind are applicable on all occasions when intellect and reason are required. An individual who emerges from the university having been exposed to a wide variety of tempting and superficially attractive bases for ordering a life, whose capacities for judgment, analysis, and selectivity have been consciously developed, is in a strong position to construct for himself, when the din and hullabaloo of the campus have been left behind, a positive ethic for a meaningful life.

Though I reject for the capable student the idea of a university as an innocuously superficial finishing school, I do see its highest function as the encouragement of the emergence of the whole man. Because I see the key to the realization of this potential in the development of the qualities of mind, integrity, and discipline, I single out these objectives as the great goal of a liberal education.

Clearly, within this framework it matters little if a man, for reasons of personal aptitude, chooses to emphasize one discipline or another during his educational experience. What is important only is that he sample a wide enough variety of subject matter so that he is called upon to exercise the faculties of reason or judgment best exploited in any one field. Thus, though I do not propose to engage professionally in any of the sciences, I consider myself fortunate for having emphasized these disciplines almost coequally with the liberal arts during the course of my high-school and college training. For though I retain only scattered fragments of the intricacies of physics, chemistry, or mathematics, the reasoned method and precise approach which they inculcated in me, and made a part of my mental equipment, have been of incalculable value subsequently.

My own educational and home background, however, has not stressed merely method and system of approach in dealing with the complexities with which we are constantly confronted. Content, especially as it relates to the ethical, cultural, and moral traditions of the religious faith of my fathers, has been a major part of my early training. The dual emphasis of my schooling on the secular and religious aspects of my intellectual and spiritual heritages has been, in the first instance, on the broad compatibility of the two, and in the second, on the necessity for a reasoned and mature approach when the irreconcilability of the two is indicated. Such occurrences, I have been taught—and in this conclusion I concur—do not argue for the relevance of the one tradition or the other. The broad system of my faith, even as our own secular heritage, is flexible enough to allow for constant reinterpretation and restructuring in the light of changing circumstances.

In the obvious and irrefutable conflict that admittedly can arise in one's dealings with a highly rational and scientific frame of reference on the one hand, and a highly subjective, emotional, spiritual context on the other, one may cite two relevant standards for judgment. In the first instance, where the mind and the temperament are disturbed by a conflict of teaching, a reordering of values is indicated so that a new equilibrium position may be reached. Secondly, the realism and maturity to which I referred at the beginning of this essay demand a recognition that inherent in the order of the universe is contradiction, and that every man must make peace with the idea that there is unavoidable conflict between his objective reason and the subjective qualities of the human personality. My decision to eat candy, though I know I should not, is not a mark of wickedness or stupidity. It is, rather, some would say, an act of folly; others might call it a sign of weakness, still others a lack of self-discipline. All, however, recognize that the act represents a triumph of some other capacity of the mind over the faculty of objective reason. This category of decision which, I would submit, is a constantly recurring feature of our lives, represents, practically, a circumscription over the exercise of pure reason. Some may, through rigorous training or discipline, widen the assigned area of the dispassionate capacities of the mind. For all, to a greater or lesser extent, however, there is a twilight zone that separates the subjective and objective exercise of the human personality.

That this is so is not to be deplored, I think. I see in friends who glorify in cold calculation, who "psych everything out," who try to anticipate in every situation every eventuality, a foolishness that deprives them of the pleasure of living. For the frustration to which the inevitable failure of this preoccupation will lead in itself produces a cynicism and unhappiness incompatible with joy.

Thus, if a man be wise enough to recognize his own emotional, spiritual, and subjective needs, and be willing, despite his devotion to reason and analysis, even as he renders unto Caesar that which is Caesar's, to render unto the Lord that which is the Lord's, he may indeed be counted among the blessed.

It is not a surrender to hypocrisy to suggest, further, that a man who recognizes the inevitability of conflict between these two distinct spheres may construct two separate operational codes for specific circumstances and for dealing with specific situations. For after all, as the problem expresses itself on one level, can it not be argued that there is a dual standard in questions of faith and reason? This, I would posit, must by definition be so. For in faith we deal with what is definite and certain. In reason we concern ourselves with what can only be tentative and unsure. Thus, a man can on faith, for an illustration, accept the Biblical story of creation, while he fumbles scientifically for a verifiable hypothesis to explain the origins of life and of the earth. For in accepting the gulf that separates man from God he recognizes that though in human terms conflict between the two may seem apparent, there can ultimately be no irreconcilability of truths, and that the conception of totality of which our minds are incapable, available only to God, substantiates the reconciliation of seeming antagonisms. The problem here, after all, is little different from the disturbance of Job, who wondered about the compatibility of evil with the concept of a just God. To accept the world as it appears, using it scientifically as our frame of reference, is not to preclude the conception of infinity and perfection inherent in the God idea.

By using the conflict between faith and reason, as I see it, as an illustration of the larger struggle between subjectivity and objectivity, and the irreconcilability of the two in terms of verifiability, I do not mean to suggest the total mutual exclusion of religion and rationality. I spoke of a twilight zone, rather, where the intelligent mind must be prepared to give ground on either side as a prerequisite to intellectual and active advancement. Thus, though on one level my commitment as a Jew involves, in existential terms, a leap of faith, on a variety of others it is a question of a rational, reasoned decision that the value system, religious and ethical, that Judaism represents is for me the most intellectually satisfactory.

Yet, in a real sense, religion does indeed represent a satisfaction of the emotional, subjective qualities of our personalities. Its function, first, is to contribute to the sheer joy of living, and, second, to promote that sense of belonging and well-being that is derived from one's understanding of one's place in a bewilderingly complex world. We speak of religion as involving a very personal commitment. Surely this is true insofar as it involves the decision to believe and to accept the teachings of the faith. Yet, it is a social phenomenon as well, insofar as it relates the individual to his fellows, his environment, and the God of all men. The religious tradition of which I am a part emphasizes both of these aspects concurrently. Every phase of our existence, virtually every act of life, is ordered as part of a value system that emphasizes the wonder and uniqueness of the experience and its testimony to our dependence on a knowing God.

The influence and effect of my religious heritage on me has been profound. I am the son of an Eastern European emigrant of the early days of the century, himself born to poor and pious stock. From early childhood my father was steeped in the Jewish tradition. He attended parochial schools from dawn to late evening, where he pored over the tomes of the

Talmud, appropriating for his own the incisive qualities of mind which characterized the thought of the early fathers. He was impressed by their deep human wisdom and understanding, by their breadth of knowledge and capacities for analysis, by their limitless devotion to the ideals of a faith.

My father, thus, shared with thousands of his youthful coreligionists that sober discipline of mind and character, derived from constant study of a brilliant tradition, which emphasized obedience, virtue, and scholarship. The reverence and respect which the majesty and towering genius of the tradition evokes in all who become imbued with it made my father a convinced and committed Jew.

In the spirit of the faith, Jewish precepts pervaded all aspects of my father's life. Even his vocational choice, made after his voyage to America at the age of fifteen, was strongly influenced by the schooling of his boyhood. Surely, my father's decision to study medicine represents the kind of choice whose roots are too complex and obscure to disentangle completely. He must certainly have been moved, however, by the rabbinic literature and tradition, in which he was thoroughly grounded, which glorifies the healing art. The Talmud, for example, is replete with discussions of medical and hygienic import, and many of the early leading figures in Jewish life were practicing physicians. The outstanding philosopher of them all, for example, Maimonides, was the court physician for the king of Spain as late as the Twelfth Century.

The learning of the physician, his prestige in the larger community, the security that he enjoyed, the affinity of his role as counselor and oracle to that of the revered rabbi, lent to the profession an aura and mystique among Jews virtually unrivalled by any other. My father was doubtlessly influenced by all of these factors.

Thus, as a newly arrived immigrant, in his middle teens, with characteristic resolution my father began the secular training that would prepare him for the life of a physician.

He began his own period of "enlightenment," emphasizing secular as well as religious studies, that was to make him a man of learning and culture.

Further, despite the widening of his social orbit to include cursory contact with Gentiles, my father's primary orientation remained towards the Jewish community. He had a realistic sense, not of "his betters," but of the essential estrangement of Jew and Gentile. This estrangement, though not preventing friendly association with others, emphasizes the differences in tradition and values between the two communities. It highlights the Jewish stress on the home and the family, on scholarship and study, on faith and piety, and the subordination of all life to the revealed will of God.

This is the atmosphere in which I have been raised. Under the pressures of the anti-ritualistic American environment there have been inevitable compromises with some of the more ornate manifestations of observance. The pattern, however, that has been passed on to me, that has become so much a part of my personality, and that will be my legacy to my children, is clear: the highest development of the dispassionate, analytical qualities of mind, of integrity, and of that propriety and spiritual wisdom from which all human life worth living flows.

A LIBERAL'S PROGRESS

ABOUT A YEAR AGO, WHILE GAZING INTO the window of a bookstore, my eye fell upon a book called *The Outsider*. I immediately felt an affinity for that book, though I had no idea what lay between its covers. This attraction was a result of the fact that, almost as long as I have been truly conscious of the world around me, I have known the feeling of being in some sense an "outsider."

What is an outsider? I suppose many people think of him as a blatant rebel, with a turtle-neck sweater, baggy pants, and a perennial expression of disillusioned worldliness. Others may picture him as a meek-voiced introvert with horn-rimmed glasses. Perhaps in the generation that came to maturity in the 1930's, the outsider did in fact tend to fit these stereotypes. Today, however, he is just as likely to be indistinguishable from the up-and-coming Madison Avenue executive or the clean-cut, broad-shouldered, and tweedily dressed young Princetonian. What is it, then, that makes an outsider different, that singles him out from his fellows? Putting it most simply, we (the few of us that there are today) have not been able or have not chosen to identify *completely* with any institution or class or even creed.

The reasons for my own measure of psychological and intellectual "outsideness," as I now see in retrospect, lie in the fortuitous circumstances of my boyhood and adolescence. I was born in an Eastern metropolis, the only child of middle-class parents who were nominal members of the local Jewish community. I suppose that my parents were not terribly different from many other middle-class people, particularly middle-class Jews; yet certain characteristics of theirs, taken together, made them somewhat unusual parents and certainly proved to be major forces in the molding of the person that I now am. For one thing, thanks to the sacrifices of their own parents and their personal efforts, my parents were comparatively well educated. This meant that I was able to grow up in a home richly stocked with the works of the great thinkers of Western Civilization, a home in which the intellectual and inquiring mind was deeply revered and where the pressing problems and issues of the times were matters of daily table talk.

Equally important in the shaping of my character and personality were the political orientation and world view of which Mom and Dad were passionate devotees. I was brought up in a home where Franklin Delano Roosevelt was figuratively enshrined in a little niche in the wall of every room. The New Deal was a testament of freedom, a modern version of the human rights set forth in the Declaration of Independence. Roosevelt's enemies were evil and greedy spokesmen for a discredited past. They had to be, because President Roosevelt seemed to represent in his person all the things in which my parents believed. For example, he was the incarnation of the racial and religious tolerance which was always so important a concern in my parents' scheme of things. One of the first precepts I can actually recall my mother imparting to me was, "You must always go out of your way to be nice to a Negro." When she first said it to me, I doubt that it made much of an impression, for I had not yet experienced the bitterness of bigotry. But before many years had passed, I came to understand why my mother's usually sunny expression always became so serious when she lectured me about intolerance.

When I was about eight years old, we moved to a sleepy Southern city. Shortly after we had settled there, a young

Negro girl, who also had recently arrived from the North, came
to work for us. I remember her as a sweet, rather shy young
person. One day she went downtown to do some shopping. I
will never forget the look on her face when she returned. It
was compounded of shame, sadness and anger. Tears streamed
down her dark cheeks. When Mom asked her what had happened, the girl broke down completely. Her shoulders shook,
she sobbed so heavily. Finally the story came out. She had
gone into a grocery store and walked over to the meat counter.
When she had started to place her order, the man behind the
counter had contemptuously announced to her that he only
waited upon white people; if she wanted to buy anything, she
would have to find some white man or woman who was willing to give her order to him. Thus, our young maid—and in-
directly, I—were initiated into the United States' version of
apartheid. From that day on, bigotry was no longer something
abstract. It was tangible and worthy of hate, a thing to be
attacked whenever and wherever it appeared.

My own personal encounter with intolerance further
heightened my sensitivity to this universal problem. Once,
while on a home-hunting expedition, my parents and I were
directed by a Christian friend to a lovely house in a new
residential district. After we had been given a Cook's tour
of the place, its occupants moved to clinch the sale by assur-
ing us, in almost conspiratorial tones, that we wouldn't have
to worry about any unpleasant changes in the character of
the neighborhood; the local people carefully ran it, they explained, so that Jews were kept out. Not wanting to interfere
with the desires of the neighborhood, we found our new home
elsewhere.

I recall one evening during my first month at Princeton,
four long years ago, when I sat in a room with three new
acquaintances and heard one of them, a large, beefy fellow,
boast caustically of his psychological assaults upon two frail
Jewish boys down the hall, whom he held in deep contempt.

He told of how the previous evening he had poured water through their mail slot, until one of them, burning with indignation, had thrown open the door. For a moment he had verbally vented his wrath upon the hefty persecutor. But threatened with physical violence, he had closed the door and returned to bed, thinking, perhaps, that the Jews would always be under the shadow of *The Wall*.

My jolly acquaintance's two friends roared with mirth at the telling of this anecdote. A weak, twisted smile crossed my face. Inside I felt fury battle with fear and a profound loneliness. What does a man do in a case like that? Does he join in the general mirth and remain secure behind his companions' ignorance? Or does he leap to his feet and shout, "Well, I'm a Jew, too; what are you going to do about it?" But if one follows the latter course of action, what good does it do?

Encounter with anti-Semitism, however, does not necessarily cause an individual to become an outsider; in fact, it may well lead him inside to far closer identification with the Jewish religion and culture than he had felt before the heavy hand of prejudice had fallen on his shoulder. But this did not happen in my case. I have been drifting away from the religion of my forebears. Probably, if I had remained in the great city, surrounded by other Jews, the drift would never have begun. I would have remained a nominal member of the Jewish community, like so many other Jews, occasionally attending synagogue on a Holy Day, but generally indifferent to the religious aspect of Judaism. But I spent part of my boyhood and all of my adolescent years in a city with only a small, scattered Jewish population. From the beginning I was absorbed into the Christian community. Most of my friends were Christian and I belonged to a number of social organizations that were sponsored by Protestant Churches. Rarely during the years I lived in this city did I personally encounter overt anti-Semitism. This was, I suppose, partially due to the greater tolerance of my generation, to the seeming general decline in religious prejudice, and to the heterogeneous character of the city. Or it might be attributable to more or less fortuitous circumstances. Whatever the causes, that was what happened; so, though I had personally experienced prejudice earlier (and was destined to run into it again in the future), the alternative of complete assimilation into the Christian community lay before me as a real possibility.

Once, under the influence of a mature Protestant friend, I almost converted, but my parents objected strenuously; they were irritated by what seemed to be an intrusion in private family affairs on the part of an outsider; moreover, they still felt a kind of vague attachment to Judaism. (With many Jews this type of sentimental attachment, which comes to the fore particularly when a complete break is contemplated, may in part be a manifestation of a feeling of guilt at leaving a persecuted minority that has struggled valiantly for its existence since Biblical times.) But probably the chief explanation for my parents' objection to my definitive departure from the fold of Judaism was their feeling that I was yet too young to make a choice that reflected long, honest thought about its consequences and implications. And they were quite right in believing that I had an inadequate idea of the essential nature of either Judaism or Christianity. I had not genuinely evaluated each; and though entrance into one religion as opposed to another may be basically an act of faith, the ultimate act of faith should, it seems to me, be supported by a comprehension of the differing views of the nature of man and God that are involved.

That my parents should have recognized an eventual *right* on my part to make a *choice* as to my religious affiliation marks them out, I believe, as rather unusual parents; it also expresses the spirit of my whole upbringing. When casting about for a description of that upbringing, I inevitably come up with that oft-used and historically rich word, "humanistic." How does this basic and traditional concept of modern Western Civilization apply to the upbringing of *this* young man of the Twentieth Century? It applies most fundamentally in the sense that I grew up believing that the goods of this world are man's chief concern, that his victories and defeats, his joy and his anguish, are experienced here on earth and are a consequence of his interaction with his fellows and his environment, and that man, therefore, is essentially the master of his own destiny.

Thinking about it now, I wonder whether one might not also call my boyhood "the education of a liberal," for most of the canons of liberalism were deeply embedded in my mind long before I came to Princeton. Education as a panacea, the rationality and probable perfectibility of man, the value and desirability of the most direct form of democracy possible in any given situation, the ideal of the rational and scientific approach to life, contempt for useless tradition, dislike of aristocracies—all were elements in my conception of life and the world. I was a devotee not only of traditional liberal ideology, but also of modern liberal politics. All conservatives were, in my mind, selfish, vicious, or stupid. I was an ardent supporter of that medley of governmental programs designed to help our society's lower classes.

My childhood inculcation with the philosophy of humanism and the values of liberalism was not, however, a matter of any compulsive educational preoccupation on the part of my folks. They never seemed to deem it necessary to pound these values and concepts into my young, malleable mind. In fact, for the most part, Mother and Dad were extremely permissive parents. Their more or less conscious goal was to get me to think for myself, to use my mind to its fullest capacity, to become an autonomous individual capable of purposive, carefully considered action. Even in that very sensitive area of morals, they did not fall prey to the understandable temptation to threaten dire evil and terrible punishment for deviations from their norms. A great deal of my moral education, in fact, was provided by their own actions. They never resorted either to the promise of heaven or the threat of hell. To put it colloquially, I was taught to be good for goodness' sake, rather than specifically for God's sake. And when I think about it, the almost incredible thing is that my parents' moral examples and precepts have stuck and continue to stick with me. Even now that I am aware of the fact that my conscience is the product of my upbringing (this is not to deny the possibility that the stuff of which conscience is made is God-implanted), I am still faithful to the dictates of that conscience. I am repelled by a lie; I even avoid the so-called "white lie," unless it is quite clear that the truth will injure an innocent human being. If I were to lie to protect myself, I know that I would feel the utmost self-contempt. I know, because in the few cases I have done so, I have regarded myself with a deep sense of loathing.

Because of this powerful and sensitive moral and social conscience that was built into me during my youth, I have been increasingly disturbed by the manifold signs in America of widespread disregard of, and contempt for, traditional ethical and moral standards. Juvenile delinquency; assaults upon men, women and children; the wanton destruction of property; and youthful irresponsibility in general have reached more and more alarming proportions and seem to be on the increase with each year that passes. What is happening to the so vitally necessary built-in moral basis of our democratic society?

Nor is moral and ethical myopia today restricted to the youth of America. The realm of public affairs is one area where it has been particularly obtrusive. Political rhetoric could not grovel much more deeply in the mud than it does now—on both sides of the party fence. How many of our public figures have, for a fistful of votes, been willing unjustly to ruin other men's reputations! I have no illusions about the temptations of politics. I know that the art of government has always and everywhere involved a good deal of smut. What troubles me the most is the apparent willingness of educated and ordinarily responsible people to throw away their ethics when they enter the realm of public affairs, and the indifference of most of the electorate to grossly unethical campaign practices. In many cases the voter is not even aware that they are unethical. If he were, they probably wouldn't be used.

Another phenomenon which expresses the erosion of moral standards and the sense of social responsibility in our society is a type of personality which is all too often overlooked— the bohemian intellectual. He is the fellow who is determined to prove that he is an individualist. And what queer forms his proof often takes. They vary from growing a goatee, to wearing ill-fitting, creased clothes, to assuming a calculated indifference to the amenities of life such as saying "good morning" or avoiding those barbs of superfluous, sarcastic wit that injure feelings and stultify social gatherings. This individual is wholly egocentric; he is blissfully unaware of, or disinterested in the great social, political, and economic problems that weigh upon our world. One of his chief forms of pleasure is "America-baiting." You name it, and if it is bad, it can be found in America. Conformity? Why, every American except this fellow and a few of his confreres has the individuality of a docile cow. Materialism? Why, Americans are the crassest materialists imaginable, interested only in building bigger and better machines. While everything in America is bad, everything in Europe is usually good. If you ask him (or even if you don't) this joyfully cynical individual will tell you that the best women, cars, paintings, movies, ad nauseam, are to be found in England or on the continent. And as for the things of the spirit, why there is simply no comparison. What a jolting and resented experience it is for our bohemian intellectual when you suggest that the French, for example, have not been very rational or spiritual in their handling of the Algerian mess. If you really want to arouse him, just suggest that the European intellectuals have become culturally bankrupt and morally decadent and have often lost their nerve in the bargain. His answer, of course, will be another diatribe against America.

Somewhat akin to the bohemian intellectual is the intellectual in search of his soul. This poor chap seems to be perpetually in a state of agony. He is desperately looking for meaning in his life and is usually quite unconcerned about the people over whom he runs in the course of his travels. It is not surprising to see him fluctuating between two extremes: on the one hand, the complete denial of authority and traditional standards, or, on the other, acceptance of some unitary authoritarian system that relieves him of the burden of making moral choices and of continued searching for the meaning of life. If only the intellectual in search of his soul were a bit more concerned about other people's souls and bodies, I would be a good deal more sympathetic towards him. But this does not mean that I am enamored of that opposite kind of subjectivist—the pious and irrepressible soul-saver. What bothers me about him is his almost inevitable tendency quickly to become a victim of overweening pride in his own goodness; and even more undesirable and even dangerous is his readiness to forget that man has a body and earthly responsibilities as well as a soul. Our current wave of mass evangelism may be a fine thing in many ways. I would feel much better about it, however, if I could be sure that, besides being sincere, the soul-savers concerned had really thought through the implications of what they were attempting and of the responses they were getting. For a society, as for an individual, there must be a mean between the sanctimonious and the amoral.

Another related facet of the problem of law and morality in contemporary American Civilization is the apparently ever-growing tendency, particularly on the part of psychologists, psychiatrists and sociologists (although the phenomenon has begun to seep into the general public as well), to take anti-social conduct much less seriously than it should be taken and to try to rationalize it away. A man robs a bank and kills a policeman who attempts to stop him. We are told that the man was a "product" of the "junglelike" environment of the slums. Another man rapes and kills a girl; but we are told that he is the offspring of a broken family or that he simply is sick and needs care. We are often so busy understanding why a crime has been committed that we forget that an evil attack has been made upon civilized society, an attack that should be severely punished. Please don't misunderstand me. I am not lashing out at the genuine attempts being made to discover the motivation of crime. Such attempts are most important if society is to fare better in reducing crime. What disturbs me is the failure of some to couple understanding with just anger and deserved and appropriate punishment.

What, I have often asked myself and discussed with my friends, are the roots of our loosening morality? The most important, it seems to me, is the very nature of our individualistic, utilitarian, and pragmatic order of things. Beginning with our economic relationships, more and more aspects of our society have been rationalized, that is, have come to be measured and governed by the sole criterion of, "What's the percentage?" —either for the individual or for the society. This has, it is true, made our society much freer and more open and democratic than any other in history; in so doing, however, it has also weakened the traditional, built-in ethical commitment which, whether we realized it or not, made our development of freedom and democracy possible. As a result, deprived of the aura of universality, permanence, "naturalness," and religious sanction that once surrounded them, our institutions and beliefs no longer command the respect and veneration of Americans that I think they once did. Of course, I would readily admit that far from *all* Americans respected the letter and spirit of our traditional moral precepts in the past; and it is a fact that there are plenty of Americans today (including myself) who continue to be profoundly attached to them. The whole thing is a matter of degree, but degrees can make a great deal of difference.

By thus alluding to the pragmatic, materialistic aspirations of Americans, I may appear to be joining the refrain that is constantly on the lips of so many foreigners, especially from Europe, the Middle East, and Asia. The gist of this familiar anti-American refrain is that Americans are crass and egoistic worshippers of Mammon. It has always struck me as funny, in this regard, that the people who shout the loudest about our alleged materialism are often the same people who are trying the most desperately to obtain economic aid from us so that they too can eventually enjoy all the material luxuries that we possess. Frankly, I am a wee bit weary of hearing, for example, Asian and French intellectuals telling us so smugly of the spiritual superiority of *their* societies. The Asians are so spiritual that many of them seem on the verge of selling their birthright of freedom to the Communists in the hope of finding some short cut to industrialization. And spiritual France is the nation that, before the Nazi psychological and military onslaught in World War II, bent like a weak reed. The superficial, materialistic and naïve Americans, on the other hand, are the people who after both World Wars poured truly vast sums of money and quantities of foodstuffs into Europe to save millions of men, women and children from starvation. We are the people who *gave* independence to the Philippines. We are the people who have provided most of the cash for UNICEF and UNESCO. And we are the people who have been distributing economic aid to practically the whole world. In part, I admit, our actions have been motivated by self-interest. But many of our acts of humanity predated the cold war by years and certainly, it seems to me at least, expressed a genuine idealism and altruism. If, therefore, one really wants to compare spiritual dedication, the United States, I would maintain, can hold its own with any nation. Lovers of the goods of this life we are; but this need not and does not mean that we have lost sight of the more intangible humane goods of the human situation.

It may seem surprising to find me singing the praises of American society when, above, I was so critical of so many things. Well, just as I'm not blind to the faults of the girl whom I love, I'm not blind to the faults of my country. I guess the trouble is that often, when talking about the things one is really attached to, one takes the good qualities for granted and simply points an impatient finger at the less enviable attributes. So perhaps, at this point, I should mention some of the things about our society, and especially my own generation, which I find good and even admirable.

For one thing, I think that we are, as a whole, a rather tolerant people. True, we have had and still have plenty of black marks in this area. But, I would insist, we have been steadily improving. The very secularism, relativism, and even materialism about which I expressed such mixed feelings above, have probably done most of all to wear down provincial ignorance and prejudice. My generation, for example, is more tolerant of all kinds of minorities than were previous ones. My generation is also, I might add, more realistic than its predecessors. For instance, we seem much better prepared to face up to and shoulder the burdens of an excruciatingly long cold war. The reason for this is that we are probably the first generation of Americans who have some inkling of the price of democracy in the world as it is, and who have once and for all lost the illusion that there are any quick or total solutions to the grave problems that face us. Another significant thing about us, I would say, is that we have at least partially escaped the clutches of the Horatio Alger myth. Most of my fellow Princetonians would prefer a comfortable salary, good health, and a happy family life to a million dollars plus ulcers, added to the possibility of an empty and neglected home. A very considerable number of Princetonians (who in this respect, at least, are not atypical, I suspect) are looking forward to entering professions that are not particularly lucrative but which promise their practitioners a real chance at socially useful, soul-satisfying and creative work, professions such as the foreign service, teaching, the ministry, and journalism.

One of the most serious charges often levelled at my generation and at Americans generally is that we are terrible conformists, that we have lost our grip on our individuality. I have worked this problem of conformity over and over again in my mind; I have spent many an evening discussing it. Many people here at Princeton are especially sensitive on this subject. The reason, of course, is that Princeton men are often regarded by some of their more detached classmates and by others who have not passed through these ivied halls as glaring manifestations of the conformist trend in our society. That certain patterns do exist here at Princeton to which a majority of the students adhere cannot be denied. This holds most obviously in the area of dress. Some of our hereditary tweeds (the boys who were born with Black Watch plaid diapers on) take cynical pleasure in the metamorphosis in attire which is undergone by some of those who have not come to Princeton from the rarefied atmosphere of the preparatory school. On the first Sunday of Freshman year these latter can be seen marching into Chapel with padded shoulders, one or two buttons on their jackets, wide shirt collars, and thin knitted ties. Then, after a few months have gone by, behold the transformation. Padding has disappeared from the shoulders, every suit has three buttons, collars have been narrowed or are held down by buttons or tabs, and the thin knit tie has been replaced by a stately foulard. Humorous as this may be, the question is, is it pernicious? Does it stunt a man's intellectual growth? Does it erode his moral values? Does it deprive him of some aspect of his humanity? I think not. Adherence to the

Ivy League norm in clothes (which, regardless of popular misconceptions, leaves very considerable leeway for the expression of individual preferences) is, like many other examples of contemporary conformity, a Lilliputian threat to meaningful individualism, if it is a threat at all. After all, a man's uniqueness and spiritual autonomy and independence are matters of his mind, his personality, and his emotions. So far as I am concerned, therefore, the only varieties of conformity really worthy of censure and concern are those which impress on men and women prescribed and prefabricated values and thoughts and which, thereby, relieve them of the necessity and the opportunity of judging by and following the dictates of their own minds and consciences.

Unfortunately, with our present lack of deep and widespread economic grievances and with our ever-expanding and highly scientific political as well as economic advertising, we can find all too many examples of this damaging kind of conformity in our society. Yet as much as we must be alert to and resist this phenomenon wherever we find it, our concern, I would suggest, should be tempered by such common-sense considerations as the following. Is not a high measure of voluntary and even unconscious conformity a precondition for the very existence of society? Is this not particularly so in a free society such as the United States, a society which hopes to live as much as possible without *imposed* authoritarian order and regimentation? And with all our conformity, is it not almost insignificant when compared, say, with the blind traditionalism in thought and action of history's great peasant masses?

Perhaps the most reassuring thing about conformity in the United States is that, at least among the fairly sizable educated groups in this country, the individual is aware of his conforming. Ours is an age of introspection and self-evaluation. We are constantly probing the most enshrouded depths of our subconscious as well as our conscious. We may conform, but we know it. Unlike many other peoples, we have succeeded in isolating our basic assumptions and can see ourselves in some reasonably broad perspective.

The key problem with conformity as with most of the other threats to our traditional way of life is, it seems to me, this. With the educated and self-aware being in a minority, how do you inculcate the values and sensitivities of the intellectual community in the mass of the people? How do you obtain their enduring support for the open society? How do you protect them and the nation from the Coughlins, the Longs, and the McCarthys? And, while winning their support or acquiescence in the open society, how do you build into them that sense of discipline and respect for law which is the *sine qua non* for the durability of liberal democracy?

The problem, I believe, must be dealt with on at least three levels—education, the family, and the church. I think that our primary and secondary schools must serve, far more adequately than they are doing today, as major means for instilling in the youth of America a sense of the grandeur of our political institutions. Reverence of and affection for the Constitution should characterize the thinking of every schoolboy. Our unique form of government should be clad in hallowed clothes. The Constitutional Fathers should be placed on even higher pedestals than they currently occupy. (Economic interpretations of the Constitution, I would add, are not fit intellectual fodder for young minds that have not yet been attached firmly to faithful adherence to all that is best in our tradition.) Would this be hypocrisy? No. I sincerely believe that the Constitution is one of the greatest documents ever struck off by the mind of man, regardless of the motives of its creators.

Strict adherence to law as such should also be part of the intellectual inoculation of America's youth. The flaccid permissiveness of much education in America at the lower levels must be eliminated. "Modern" education has gone too far. Discipline in regard to both curricula and administration must be tightened up. I am, however, definitely in favor of retaining at least two elements that can be found in many modern educational curricula. These are, firstly, intercultural education designed to reduce racial and religious tensions among Americans (which will also be reduced as our sense of an American nationality further develops), and, secondly, international study programs.

Since some of these conservative reform proposals appear to substantiate a number of the charges levied at our public schools by genuine conservatives as well as by Neanderthalic extremists on the Right, many liberals may find them shocking either in tone or implication. My only answer is that reforms such as these are necessary as bulwarks of moderate conservatism as well as liberalism in their joint multi-fronted struggle to hold back the authoritarianism of the Right as well as the Left.

In developing a respect for law and tradition among the youth, the school must have the co-operation of the family. Discipline within the family must be heightened and enforced, not so much as to ideas but above all in the realm of action and conduct. And in the performance of this task the family can and should be assisted in a number of ways by the community: by the provision of more extensive organized recreation, by the banning of the plethora of degenerate and polluting comic books and pulp magazines, by the imposition of urban curfews for boys and girls, and by making it more difficult, especially for juveniles with a record of delinquency, to obtain a driver's license.

The churches also have an important role to play in improving the moral and ethical condition of our society. In spite of the drastic loosening of the bonds of faith that have occurred over the past few centuries, the vast majority of Americans still adhere at least nominally to some organized church or religion. At least once a week these millions of citizens are reminded of the ties that bind them to God and to other human beings. Here is a type of sanction for socially dedicated and ethical behavior which must be recognized and strengthened.

My growing realization of the value of religious belief for our open society, and probably for any free people, has assisted in moving me to come to terms with my own personal religious problems. During high school, my religious position was basically one of indifference, occasionally punctuated by a mild feeling of yearning or hostility. Gradually, as I was drawn more and more into the Christian community, and as I experienced some of the essential spirit of Christianity on occasions such as Christmas, my sense of yearning increased. Because my parents and I only participated actively in the secular ritual, for example, I had a feeling of being a little left out at Christmas, of being only partially embraced by it. Most Jews probably deal with the whole emotional problem presented by Christmas by focusing their spiritual energies on the Jewish festival that falls at this time (Hanukkah), but we did not celebrate it. The reason we didn't, I think, was because it had no meaning for us, particularly for me. Our own experience in this regard seems to me to be a microcosm of the fundamental problems that confront Judaism in America in general. For there are many indications that as a religion Judaism is coming to have less and less meaning for the bulk of American Jewry. Almost all of the varied Jewish holidays commemorate secular events. For some Jews these events have less emotive force than the great American secular holidays such as July Fourth, Memorial Day, etc. The number of Jews who feel this way is almost bound to grow as the process of cultural assimilation continues.

Like all religions, Judaism has been injured by ritualistic and dogmatic anachronisms which just don't seem very relevant to the American scene. One example of this in Judaism is the dietary laws. The majority of American Jews have attempted to deal with this problem by discarding various facets of Jewish practice and belief. But, having dropped one type of burden, they have found themselves encumbered by a new one —the loss of identity. Since Judaism has been a culture as well as a religion, the religion becomes less distinctive when its cultural prescriptions are eschewed.

It seems to me that Judaism is increasingly in danger of losing its identity as a genuine religion the more it Americanizes itself, the more it modifies its practices in conformity with the established patterns of American culture. Yet, if it attempts to return to a new orthodoxy, how can it help but leave behind the majority of American Jews who will find orthodoxy something peculiar and alien and who, moreover, understandably have no desire to suffer the psychological tortures of the unassimilated, the strange, and the different. Should they be condemned for a disinclination to become martyrs? I think not. If Judaism still had a *unique* contribution to make to Western Civilization, I would, perhaps, reply in the affirmative. But I do not think that such is the case. There can be no question that Judaism *has made* contributions to Western Civilization that are not only distinctive but of incalculable value. These contributions are part of the warp and woof of our culture, and this is a fact of great significance. This means, however, that since Judaism's contributions are an integral part of our civilization, there is no danger that they would be dissipated if the Jewish religion were to disappear as a distinct entity.

In regard to my own religious proclivities, the above discussion has been little more than academic. Judaism has not satisfied my own unique spiritual hunger, mild though it has been. It was not only during Christmas (and to a lesser extent Easter) that I experienced such yearnings. My entire first year at Princeton was a year during which I often felt an agony of spirit. Though I had been popular and successful in high school, my self-confidence wilted the first day I set foot on

Princeton's campus. The fact that dozens of my classmates had also been the academic leaders of their high schools and preparatory schools seemed to be drummed into my mind constantly. I failed to be selected for the Princeton Freshman Council; memories of past glory mocked me. My roommates were strangers and remained so for a long time. I had neither parents, relatives, nor close friends to whom I could turn. I was the only man from my high school to attend Princeton. No member of the faculty, including my advisor, appeared particularly interested in me as an individual. So, I turned to prayer. Every night, before I went to bed, I knelt on the bare wooden floor of my room, knitted my fingers together, closed my eyes and prayed to an unknown god for advice, wisdom, and guidance.

My daily spiritual and emotional catharsis helped me through that first difficult year. Whether my general pleas for aid and guidance were heard and answered by an omnipotent and omniscient being, I don't know. I don't even know, nor do I ever expect to know, whether such a being does in fact exist. Yet those prayers helped to sustain me and my values and my individuality in a time of mental travail. I prayed less often after that, and rarely pray now, but I am no longer indifferent to the value of prayer and of spiritual communion. I have concluded, moreover, that the act of communion should not always be an isolated, solitary event. By participating in an organized religious body this experience can be shared with others. At least one of the humanly and socially useful benefits to be derived from participating with others in the rites of religion is an enhanced feeling of connection with and responsibility for one's fellows. In other words, the conscience is strengthened, and in the never-ending battle between the ethical and egocentric elements in man, a powerful lance is thus forged for the former.

I must explain, at this point, that my concern with ethics, religion, and society is, as with most other Americans, juxtaposed against a great deal of personal ambition. In fact, the desire for wealth, power, and prestige probably burns more brightly in me than in many of my confreres. My ambition is probably explicable in terms of the values of our culture and in terms of my particular circumstances. Coming from a middle-class family that lived well because it lived from day to day, rarely putting any money aside and still able to taste only some of the pleasant and expensive luxuries which our industrial plant provides, I have no illusions about the desirability of having money. While some of life's most precious gifts, as for example, love, cannot be bought, many of the things that will go into shaping a full and happy life for me cost a good deal of money. I like large and beautiful homes surrounded by wide expanses of green lawn and artfully constructed flower beds. I like books; even now I find it difficult to walk into a bookstore without making at least one purchase. Several of the sports I enjoy most involve considerable expense. So do travelling and the theater. And, of course, money is one key for the attainment of prestige.

Far more than money, however, I want to participate in the making of the tremendous decisions that are going to shape the future of the United States and the world. Altruistic and egoistic motives, inextricably intertwined, underlie this more pressing ambition. I want to occupy an important position in our government so that I can help to improve the situation of mankind. It will give me great joy if I can alleviate the suffering of some people and bring at least a little joy to others. Political power provides a man with many means for achieving these purposes. I also hope to serve as a leader of society because the role almost guarantees me a creative, dynamic, and meaningful life that will be terminated only by death. The thought of useless retirement, of spending my declining years apart from the flux of events, in the company of other old and useless men, frightens and disheartens me. I am determined to remain useful to the end.

My desire to achieve success, particularly in the political realm, will undoubtedly come into conflict from time to time with my ethical and moral sense. The path of the demagogue or the hypocrite is well trod and often offers inviting short cuts which can be rationalized by saying to oneself that the end justifies the means. The values inculcated in me by my parents will help to strengthen my will, as will, I suspect, active participation in some organized religion. And I want the girl whom I eventually marry to assist me in rejecting the unethical temptations that abound in public life. She should serve as a loving conscience, a living reminder of my basic values. I definitely don't want a wife who will rubber-stamp every decision I make. Of course, I hope that the woman I marry will be an asset to my career. I am sure she will be if she embodies the abstract qualities which I value in a woman —sweetness, moral strength, the capacity for great compassion, an alert mind, intellectual curiosity, and (before you think me inhuman) a pretty face and a shapely body. I assume that my wife will not possess all of these qualities to the fullest extent desirable; I doubt that any woman could. But she will embody some of them. I will never marry a woman who would base her happiness on my success, who lacks sweetness and compassion, or who would measure out her life in cocktail glasses.

When I began this little public journey into myself, I called myself an outsider. You may still be wondering why, for I have not explicitly described in detail all the elements that comprise my sense of detachment. However, some of you may have detected them woven into the fabric of my thoughts. The source of my religious outsideness is clear. Even when (and if) I enter a particular church, I doubt that I will ever completely lose some sense of detachment. Nor is it likely that I will ever adhere completely to the political and philosophical dogmas of either liberalism or conservatism. And even if I obtain wealth and prestige, and in so doing enter the upper class, I will not be mentally absorbed. I will always quietly pride myself on my ability to be in and yet a little out of all the channels which life provides for a man's mind, body, and soul. And it may not be presumptuous to think that I will be of greater service to my country and my fellow human beings at least in part because of my detachment. Detachment, I believe, can be a most precious gift, especially when it is not accompanied by alienation from the society.

I would like to say, in conclusion, that my happiness is drawn from many sources: from the few girls I have loved and the many I have liked; from the friends I have made; from the kindred spirits I have communed with in the past and from the prospect of those whom I may meet in the future; I find pleasure in a well-placed tennis shot or a walk in the warm spring air along the quiet residential streets of Princeton. In the future I look forward to intellectual endeavor and political strife. I will know success and failure. I will experience temptation; sometimes I will fall like Adam, but then I hope to recover and stand strong. And always my way will be lighted by my vision of the good society, a community of free men, a community with liberty and order, a community in which the open, inquiring mind shall be the rule rather than the exception. Such a vision is, to my mind, worth striving for. It will always provide meaning for my life.

THE THIRD EYE

IF I WERE TO TRY TO FIND SOME ICON for my generation, I would look for a mythical creature with three eyes, one of which was detached from the head and always at a respectable distance from the body. We are the generation of the third eye, the eye of self-consciousness, the eye of self-criticism. Whatever we do is subject to its gaze; when we are sad, it mocks the poses we assume; and when we are gay, it does not share our levity but seems to smirk, like Shakespeare's Thersites, with the shame of it all. This mythical creature would live in constant fear of his third eye. When he would start to laugh, he would catch sight of it; and the laugh would die in his throat, leaving a silly, silent grin on the creature's face. If he should be in love, the third eye would be a duenna enforcing not the body's but the mind's chasity—the body might be full in love, the mind never. Yet the creature should guard his third eye jealously. All attempts to sever the eye from him, by political creed, by personal attachment, by complete loyalty to any entity beyond the self, would be resisted mightily; for this creature would have lost the illusion of spontaneity.

The characteristic fear of our generation is our horror of finding ourselves ludicrous. We may recognize that ludicrousness is the cost of sincere venture in any field; but, always measuring beforehand the possibility of our own unsuccess, we protect ourselves against the exposure that comes with failure. The third eye looks enviously at past history, finding there not precedents but warnings. Our jealousy, now, is for the Twenties. We, seeds sown in the first planting after the Depression's dearth, see in that decade a time when investment and commitment, in stocks or in creeds, was possible. We envy the dizziness of speculation that was the trope of the whole period. We envy—without daring to imitate—our fathers' freedom to join Communist cell groups, to cultivate Dadaist fads, to commit themselves to any of the fragmented creeds that were bound to fail. With us, the dizziness is necessarily gone. A Federal Reserve System of the Imagination is with us to protect us from our parents' glorious flop. Hindsight is a mixed blessing.

The reason our generation has been accused of quietude is probably because our elders are afraid of our image, when they compare it to their own. We are accused of not being rebellious enough. But our elders have done the rebelling for us. *Their* present point of view, created in their own old age, coincides so nicely with *our* present point of view, created in our youth, that the myth of the son's rebellion against the father seems to have exhausted itself.

Even the spirit of criticism has risen to such a pitch in us that it looks sardonically at its own operation. Our attitude towards Oliver Wendell Holmes might illustrate this paradox of criticism turned against itself. In Holmes's age, we recognize, his skepticism was a creative force. It was the cathartic to the obstinacy of his contemporaries. In our age, his precepts are so general that their author goes unrecognized by the generation which practices them; and, thus, of themselves, they have no saving grace. His awareness of the prevalence of unreason in law went a long way in the eradication of that fertile source of history's constructive or destructive energy. "To have doubted one's own first principles," we quite agree, "is the mark of the civilized man." We have kept his doubt, but lost his abiding certitude in either the necessity or the efficaciousness of doubt. We are grateful for his part in the destruction of the unreasonable absolute; but we are becoming agonizingly conscious of the need for an absolute that will stand up to his pragmatic tests.

The third eye operates less subtly when we look to the Thirties for patterns of behavior to imitate. Most of our parents make a hero or a scapegoat of President Roosevelt, and recognize no moderate point of view towards him. Young Democrats and Republicans alike, *our* attitude towards him is so tolerant as to be destructive of his image, either the good one or the bad one. Democrats praise him, not as the visionary intellect of our time, but as a masterful politician with a grasp of actuality that accidentally transcended the opportunism which marked his character. Republicans on college campuses no longer accuse him of being a "European collectivist"; rather, they take him to task for *not* transcending his characteristic opportunism, for trying to extend the executive prerogative beyond the White House to the Supreme Court. In a typical campus political bull session, nowadays, both parties agree that, whether or not Hoover might have done the job equally well, Roosevelt was the best friend American business ever had, that he saved the United States for capitalism, and that he was essentially a bourgeois at heart. Thus the fervor of social responsibility of the Thirties dies a quiet death on today's college campus, another victim of an obsessively historical and analytical point of view.

Perhaps this is so because we have seen so many of the intellectual leaders of that day recant. John Dos Passos, for one, serves as the most useful image of a generation ashamed of itself and anxious to dismiss its history. In 1936, Dos Passos, eulogizing Veblen, gave clear voice to an era with heroes and villains equally well defined. On the one hand, he saw "A warlike society strangled by the bureaucracies of the monopolies forced by the law of diminishing returns to grind down more and more the common men for profit," on the other, "a new matter of fact society dominated by the needs of men and women who did the work and the incredibly vast possibilities for peace and plenty offered by the progress of technology." That we have since found such a comfortable set of alternatives practically useless is less significant than the fact that the man who uttered them has taken a position with the most arch-conservative group in the country, William F. Buckley's *National Review*. No other lesson need be drawn from Dos Passos' about-face, and those of many of his contemporaries, than this: that the cost of complete commitment to his kind of social ethic recognizes no grays between its reds and whites. The old Dos Passos is no less simple-minded—and I use the term to describe his inability to handle complexities, not his mental effectiveness—than the young author of *U.S.A.* Probably, the new Dos Passos lacks the old Dos Passos' literary ability only because the present age is unprepared to accept any simplified account of its political condition, regardless of the point of view taken. Our generation has an ungovernable appetite for complexity in its intellectual heroes: this is its vice as well as its virtue. Yet were we offered the choice of which Dos Passos most appeals to us, we should all select the Dos Passos of the Thirties. In that era, before the labor groups of the country had come to their power, men like Dos Passos had the intellectual right to commit themselves to the still untested "men and women who did the work . . . and the incredibly vast possibilities for peace and plenty offered by the progress of technology." With the passage of time, *we* no longer have the intellectual right honestly to commit ourselves to a social code which reduces human problems to such simplicity.

Thus the real reason for our dislike of communism is not our fear of nonconformity or our rejection of its presumptive ungodliness. Communist principles, as we read them in the Russian publications themselves (not only in our newspapers), simply do not constitute enough of an intellectual challenge for us, the triple-eyed. A Hungarian friend of mine who met Russian soldiers on the streets of Budapest describes them as incredibly ingenuous fair-haired youngsters who mistook the Danube for the Suez Canal and readied themselves for a great battle with the American imperialist army. The Russian publications are written in ponderous, heavy prose; "bourgeois" has all the connotations of the boogy-man, and "proletarian democracy" is used as a substitute for sweetness and light. We demand a tougher and more realistic discipline than communism can possibly provide. The redeeming characteristic of my generation is a certain rigor of the intellect that, if it is without any outlet now, may someday become a truly regenerative force. At the moment, however, our disapproval of totalitarianism is not answered by a sense of pride in our own institutions. American youth, especially at Princeton, are probably the least nationalistic youth in the world. The student who travels in Europe is so anxious not to behave like the "typical" American, that his characteristic attitude towards his own country becomes apologetic rather than proud. European students set for an argument with their American counterparts discover, to their amazement, that the American student is usually most sympathetic to any critique of American foreign policy. American Jewish students travelling in Israel report that they feel a definite sense of inferiority when confronted with the typical Israeli *sabras,* whose pride in their little, besieged country often makes the American Jew ashamed of the mere fact of America's prosperity.

Thus, as critical as we are of the doctrines of the past, we are no less damagingly critical of ourselves. For humility, no generation in history exceeds our own. Just as so many of us accept the criticisms that Europeans offer of us, so we usually accept the labels applied to us by our elders. But we agree with the Europeans in order to transcend their expectation that we would *object* to their criticisms, and our willingness

to find fault with ourselves is the measure of our possibly redeeming ability to surmount the limitations of the roles imposed upon us. Conformist is the name most often given us.
Statistics are cited to prove that we are marrying earlier than
our predecessors, that we are less adventurous than our forebears, that we are more willing to accept secure jobs and settle
down in the cool suburbs than we ought to be. The statistics
are probably true, but that we recognize them as true, and
are becoming increasingly sensitive to their consequences in
our lives, promises that many of us are going to escape the
predictions set for our futures. We suspect that the great mass
of men in every age have been as mediocre as we are, but that
no age has been as *conscious* of its mediocrity as we. We talk
about conformity more than anyone else in history; we read
and write books on the subject. As a result of all this talk, increasingly large numbers of us are taking measures to protect
ourselves from it, and considering ourselves as exceptions to
the general rule.

The escape patterns of the young American intellectual
are undergoing a change unnoticed by the great majority of
his elder critics. The triple-eyed monster I described at the
beginning of this essay, I offered as our *collective* icon, but
our individual images are each slightly different, although
obedient to the same abiding convention of self-criticism. The
modes of self-expression which we are finding are more *modest,*
but perhaps much more *effective* than those resorted to in the
past. The American in the Twenties fled to Europe in order to
find sources of inspiration not available to him in America.
He went there to paint, to write, and, most frequently, to enter-
tain himself in a manner forbidden in prohibition-bound America. The Americans in the Fifties go to Europe to study, usually
on a Fulbright or some other form of fellowship grant. If we
are usually willing to criticize America when abroad, we are
less willing to *despise* America, probably because we cannot

help remembering that American tax money usually provides the means to our education. Nor do many of us cherish the notion of permanently escaping our national institutions, however many defects we may see in them.

Organizational science, in all levels of our society, may soon guarantee a more adequate livelihood for all educated men, and money is already becoming less and less of a factor in the choice of occupation. With the other factors—patriotism, social responsibility, religious duty—also gone or going, the work itself, whatever it is, may absorb more and more of the energies formerly directed elsewhere. A pride in the assigned task carefully done may be enough of a morality to replace all the others that in our self-consciousness we find useless. The university is traditionally the place where the work of the mind, scholarship, has always been honored as an end in itself; and the responsible graduate has often been able to absorb enough of his teachers' mental rigor to wish to imitate them. Moreover, the essential requirement of scholarship, or of any work that can be considered as an end in itself, is that the subject's own personality be considered secondary to the problem at hand. Thus, what begins as a disease of the imagination, the self-consciousness that frustrates action, may eradicate itself when it is stripped away before an impersonal consideration of the intricacies of specific work-problems. Self-criticism, instead of preventing creative work, will operate as a rigor strengthening such work, once the impossible expectations of earlier ages have been eliminated. Sidney Hook once defined maturity as the possession of rational expectations. In regard to past motives of behavior, our third eye is destructive of irrational expectations. In regard to future motives of behavior, the third eye may discover those limited and realizable forms of creative action that will survive all the tests our critical consciences can pose.